Sanjeev Kapoor's

COOKING WITH
OLIVE OIL

In association with Alyona Kapoor

PopulaR prakashan

www.popularprakashan.com

Published by

Popular Prakashan Pvt. Ltd.

301, Mahalaxmi Chambers

22, Bhulabhai Desai Road

Mumbai 400 026

for KHANA KHAZANA PUBLICATIONS PVT. LTD.

(4245)

ISBN 978-81-7991-497-7

Book Design	:	Indivisual
Photography	:	Bharat Bhirangi & Aarti Manik
Aesthetics	:	Aarti Manik
Food Styling	:	Khana Khazana India Pvt. Ltd.
		Trupti Kale
Typeset by	:	Bhaskar & Megha

PRINTED IN INDIA

Ajanta Offset & Packagings Ltd.

New Delhi-110 002

AUTHOR'S NOTE...

My tryst with olive oil began in New Zealand in 1989. I was the Executive Chef of an Indian restaurant with a handful of Indian cooks helping out. The kitchen was huge, so I suggested to the owner that two restaurants could be easily run from it. That was the start of another restaurant serving international cuisine.

Ingredients were ordered and as the kitchen was same, it was natural to use them without much deliberation. As I took inventory at the end of the month, I realised that the consumption of olive oil had increased. What was happening? The Indian cooks had been using it for Indian food! Then it struck me. There was no resistance from traditional cooks to using a new cooking medium. What's more there was no resistance from the patrons either. It was evident that cook and consumer both were comfortable with Indian food cooked in olive oil.

It was the same story at home. We had a few bottles of different kinds of olive oil remaining from a New York food festival. I had casually put them away on our kitchen shelf. A few months later, I wanted to use one particular brand of olive oil in a recipe. But what did I find? Our cook, a dear 78-year-old lady from Andhra Pradesh who has been with us for many years, had used it all up. She did not find it difficult to use. It did not matter to her what oil she was using. And we did not notice any change in taste at the table either!

Knowing that olive oil is the best oil for health, we have switched. And believe me, these teaspoons of liquid gold do a lot to keep your heart healthy. The recipes in Cooking with Olive Oil have been well-researched. The book is a one-stop guide to using olive oil in all types of Indian cuisine. This sort of adaptation has been unheard-of till now. But the fact remains: Indians need to shape up what with the rising rates of heart disease, obesity and diabetes. India has the highest incidence of these lifestyle diseases in the world.

I don't see any challenge in adapting something as healthy as olive oil in Indian cooking. Indian food is already replete with goodness of indigenous herbs and spices and all that remains is to add the goodness of olive oil so that it can be taken to the next level of health.

A Mediterranean legend goes that anyone who planted an olive grove expected to live long because olive trees took so many years to mature.

I firmly believe that if we cook with olive oil we too, can look forward to a long and healthy life!

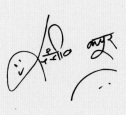

All about Olive Oil

Virgin olive oil is the oily juice of the olive fruit. It is obtained exclusively by mechanical or other physical procedures in conditions, particularly temperature conditions, which do not cause its deterioration. The only treatments involved are fruit washing, crushing, preparation of the olive mash or paste, separation of the solid and liquid phases, decanting and/or centrifuging and filtration.

Oil quality is determined by many equally important factors during olive cultivation and the subsequent stages of harvesting, storage and processing.

Appropriate care of the olive trees is needed to make them bear large crops of good quality fruit. Harvest timing depends on whether the olives are going to be made into olive oil or used as table olives. As oil accumulates in the olive fruits and their moisture content decreases, they turn from green to purple, and then to varying shades of black. Fruitier olive oils are obtained if the olives are harvested when they start to ripen, even if quite a large percentage of the olives are still green. Bringing forward or putting back harvesting gives oils with very different fragrances and tastes. After they have been delivered to the mill, the olives have to be sorted and washed. They should be crushed as quickly as possible because fermentation occurs very rapidly and can have a big impact on product quality. In the olden days, the olive fruits were crushed in stone mills operated by man or animal power; nowadays, machines are used.

After the olives are crushed, the olive paste is mixed slowly and continuously to prepare it for subsequent separation of the liquid and solid phases by different extraction methods. In the final stage, the product undergoes very strict quality controls.

What are the Types of Olive Oil?

Olive oil is the oil obtained solely from the fruit of the olive tree (Olea europaea L.), to the exclusion of oils obtained by solvents or re-esterification processes and of any mixture with oils of other kinds. It is marketed according to the designations (names) and definitions listed below:

1. Virgin Olive Oils

Virgin olive oil is the oil obtained from the fruit of the olive tree solely by mechanical or other physical means under conditions, particularly thermal conditions, that do not lead to alterations in the oil, and which have not undergone any treatment other than washing, decantation, centrifugation and filtration.

They are graded according to their organoleptic and chemical characteristics into the following categories:

Extra virgin olive oil: virgin olive oil with a free acidity, expressed as oleic acid, of not more than 0.8 g per 100 g and the organoleptic characteristics specified for this category.

Virgin olive oil: virgin olive oil with a free acidity, expressed as oleic acid, of not more than 2 g per 100 g and the organoleptic characteristics specified for this category.

Ordinary virgin olive oil: virgin olive oil with a free acidity, expressed as oleic acid, of not more than 3.3 g per 100 g and the organoleptic characteristics specified for this category.

2. Refined Olive Oil

This is the olive oil obtained from virgin olive oils by refining methods which do not lead to alterations in the initial glyceridic structure. Its free acidity, expressed as oleic acid, may not be more than 0.3 g per 100 g.

3. Olive Oil

This is a blend of refined olive oil and virgin olive oil fit for consumption as it is. It has a free acidity, expressed as oleic acid, of not more than 1 g per 100 g.

4. Olive-Pomace Oil

This is the oil obtained by treating olive pomace with solvents or other physical treatments, to the exclusion of oils obtained by re-esterification processes and of any mixture with oils of other kinds. Olive-pomace oil is a blend of refined olive-pomace oil and virgin

olive oils fit for consumption as they are; in no case can it be called "olive oil". It has a free acidity, expressed as oleic acid, of not more than 1 g per 100 g.

Why is olive oil healthy?

Olive is an ancient fruit worthy of the lore and acclaim that surrounds it. It yields heart-healthy olive juice, which in common parlance is known as Olive oil and satisfies all five tastes: sweet, sour, salty, bitter and pungent. Well, taste might be its biggest draw, but the talking point (especially these days) is its monounsaturated fat, which lowers cholesterol.

The effects of olive oil-enriched diets on blood lipid profile have been studied extensively. Available data reports beneficial effects in lowering triglycerides and 'bad cholesterol' that is low-density-lipoprotein (LDL) and in raising the 'good cholesterol' that is high-density-lipoprotein (HDL). Together with high blood pressure, lipid disorders are a major cardiovascular risk.

Several research findings document the important antioxidant function of the minor components of olive oil, which have major implications for the prevention of arteriosclerosis and its chief complication - myocardial infarction (heart attack) and stroke (paralytic attack).

Olive and fish oils are associated with a reduction of cancer risk, unlike oils rich in linoleic acid and possibly foods rich in saturated fat.

Olive oil-enriched diets have proven beneficial effects in treating insulin resistance and obesity. These findings have many potential implications, all of which have an enormous impact on public health. Insulin resistance and obesity are known to be involved in the pathogenesis of Type-2 diabetes, which is reaching epidemic proportions in the industrialised world and beyond.

Olive oil-enriched diets also have documented beneficial effects in lowering blood pressure levels. High blood pressure is also connected with insulin resistance and is an important cardiovascular risk factor.

Other research has focused on the effects of olive oil-enriched diets on aging. Published evidence shows that virgin olive oil, in the context of the Mediterranean diet, may prevent age-related cognitive decline and dementia. The current evidence suggests that a Mediterranean diet rich in monounsaturated oleic acid and antioxidants is associated with a significant increase in survival.

Table Olives

Ten percent of the world's olives go for table consumption. This percentage may seem small but it translates into a figure of 1,500,000 metric tonnes.

Table olive varieties are characterised by features such as good fruit size, excellent taste, a good flesh-to-stone ratio and easy detachment of the flesh from the stone.

There are three types of table olives:

Green olives: These are harvested during ripening, when they have reached normal size.

Olives turning colour: These are harvested before the stage of complete ripeness, when the olive fruits are rose to wine-rose in colour.

Black olives: These are harvested when fully or almost fully ripe.

Table olives are picked by hand because the fruit must not be damaged; however, because they are riper and come away more easily, black table olives can be harvested mechanically.

With a few exceptions, olives cannot be eaten straight from the tree owing to their strong bitterness, high oil content and low sugar content. They have to be treated in different ways, which vary according to variety and region.

Product is classified as:

Extra or Fancy, when it is top quality and free from defects.

First, Choice or Select, when it has small defects of shape, colour, skin or firmness.

Second or Standard when olives cannot be classified under either of the above categories.

After being prepared, table olives can be presented in a whole range of styles depending on their quality: whole or sliced; with or without the stone; stuffed; cracked or as a paste.

Tips on olive oil

Remember olives are fruit and virgin olive oil is a fruit juice. Air, heat and light will cause olive oil to turn rancid. If your oil has a buttery taste, then it is probably rancid. Store olive oil in a tightly sealed container away from heat and light. To maintain quality, it's a good idea to put the oil in the refrigerator during the hot months. It may appear cloudy, but this does no harm to the oil. Just bring the oil back up to room temperature to clear clouding.

Buying oil in small-sized bottles, or splitting larger bottles with friends, is a practical way to buy expensive oils. Oil purchased in bulk should always be poured into smaller containers, preferably in a can or a dark-coloured bottle. Tinted glass, porcelain and stainless steel are the best materials for containers. Olive oil should never be stored in containers made of plastic or any reactive metals.

As a natural product and unlike wine, olive oil does not improve with time, so it is best used as per the time indicated on the label of the product. Nevertheless, depending on the variety, a well-kept oil could last up to eighteen months. The colour of the oil does not determine its quality.

Cooking with olive oil

Cooking with olive oil in the Indian kitchen is simple. All you have to do is replace your traditional oil with olive oil. You can cook any recipe: be it a healthy Palak Shorba, or a Gujarati Undhiyo, an elegant Prawn Pulao or a crunchy Corn Bhel with Tomato and Olives…the list is endless. Yes, you can make the all-time favourites like Tandoori Chicken,

Kairi Murgh, Biryani, Dosa, Koki, Kabab, Upma, Laddoo, Tikki & Achar! And let us not forget the divine Shahi Tukre, Balushahi, Gujiya…

When sautéing or frying, use either a combination olive oil (one that is simply a blend of extra virgin and regular olive oil) or a straight olive oil.

Olive oil is excellent for deep-frying because it has a higher smoking point than virgin or extra virgin oils. Olive oil is ideal for frying. When heated to the right temperature, without overheating, there is no substantial change in its structure and it retains its dietary properties really well because of the antioxidants it contains and its high content of oleic acid. It has a high smoking point (210°C), well above the ideal temperature for frying food (180°C).

Another advantage of olive oil in frying is that a crust forms on the outside of the food that stops the oil from penetrating through and makes the food tastier. For this to happen the oil must be hot, so that the food is sealed and does not soak up the oil. Also there must be enough of it to make sure that the food is not burnt. Food fried in olive oil contains less fat, ideal for controlling obesity. Olive oil is, therefore, the most suitable, lightest and tastiest fat for frying.

CONTENTS...

Soups & Salads
Dal Shorba   12
Palak Shorba   15
Chicken Coconut Rasam   17
Aloo Kachalu Chaat   19
Murgh aur Shimla Mirch Salad   20
Carrot, Raisin and Black Olive Salad   23

Snacks & Starters
Tandoori Murgh Chaat   24
Tomato and Olive Upma   27
Baida Roti   28
Patra   30
Aloo ki Tikki   33
Besan Methi Cheela with Cheese   35
Angoori Prawns   36
Tandoori Chicken   39
Bhajnee Thalipeeth   41
Hara Bhara Kabab   43
Corn Bhel with Tomato and Olives   45
Mutton Shaami Kabab   47
Prawn Varuval   49
Khaas Seekh   51

Main Course
Palak Paneer   53
Aluchi Patal Bhaji   54
Aloo Posto   57
Chorchori   59
Mirchi ka Salan   61
Ker Sangri   62
Dahi Baingan   65
Undhiyo   67
Pindi Chholay   68
Gobhi Matar   71
Chana and Jackfruit Sukke   73
Baghare Baingan   74
Paneer Keema   77
Tender Coconut and Cashew Nut Sukke   79
Fish Ambotik   81
Chicken Chettinaad   83
Saagwala Gosht   85

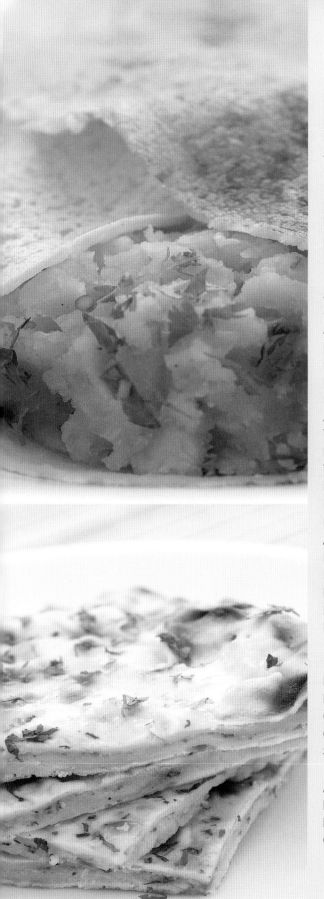

Kairi Murgh 87

Kozhi Vartha Kari 89

Shahi Korma 91

Andhra Mutton Curry 92

Gongura Chicken 95

Malabar Chemeen Kari 96

Chicken Ghassi 99

Keema Matar 101

Nalli Gosht 102

Kolhapuri Sukka Chicken 105

Accompaniments

Sabzi aur Tamatar ka Pulao 107

Aloo Anardana Kulcha 109

Gujarati Kadhi 111

Bhindi Raita 112

Murgh Biryani 115

Missi Roti 116

Amti 119

Tomato Saar 120

Kathal ki Biryani 123

Thepla 125

Kali Dal 127

Prawn Pulao 129

Koki 130

Andhra Dal 133

Lal Mirch ka Benarasi Achar 135

Hirvi Mirchicha Thecha 136

Kachche Gosht ki Biryani 139

Dosa 141

Punjabi Kadhi 143

Mithai

Balushahi 146

Besan ke Laddoo 149

Gajar aur Khajur ka Halwa 151

Gujiya 153

Shahi Tukre 154

Annexure

Measurements 156

Basic Recipes 158

Glossary 160

DAL SHORBA

INGREDIENTS

¾ cup split green gram, soaked
1 teaspoon olive oil
½ medium onion, chopped
1 inch piece ginger, chopped
3 garlic cloves, chopped
2 green chillies, chopped
½ teaspoon turmeric powder
Salt to taste
½ teaspoon roasted cumin powder
1 tablespoon lemon juice
2 tablespoons chopped fresh coriander leaves

METHOD

Heat olive oil in a deep pan. Add onion and sauté for a minute. Add ginger, garlic and green chillies. Sauté on low heat and add turmeric powder, salt, roasted cumin powder and drained *dal*. Add five cups of water. Bring to a boil and cook, on medium heat, for ten to fifteen mintues or till *dal* is very soft. Pass through a soup strainer. Bring strained *dal* to a boil and add water to adjust consistency. Continue to simmer for two to three minutes. Add lemon juice and mix. Serve piping hot garnished with coriander leaves.

A thoughtful cook can select a *dal* dish to suit any meal. The repertoire of *dal* dishes is so vast that you can make different preparations everyday, right from soups to gravies and even desserts.

PALAK SHORBA

INGREDIENTS

2 medium bunches fresh spinach leaves

2 tablespoons olive oil

3 black cardamoms

2 cloves

1 inch stick cinnamon

2 tablespoons refined flour

3 inch ginger, chopped

5 garlic cloves, chopped

1 medium onion, chopped

4-5 black peppercorns

4 bay leaves

Salt to taste

¼ teaspoon white pepper powder

1 teaspoon roasted cumin powder

METHOD

Blanch spinach leaves in boiling hot water for two to three minutes. Drain, refresh in cold water and purée them in a mixer. Heat olive oil in a deep pan. Add black cardamoms, cloves, cinnamon and refined flour and sauté for two to three minutes. Add ginger, garlic, onion and continue to sauté for about five minutes. Add black peppercorns, bay leaves, salt, white pepper powder, roasted cumin powder and five cups of water. Stir and simmer for ten minutes stirring at intervals. Strain the stock. Add the spinach purée to the strained stock and mix well. Cook for four to five minutes. Serve piping hot.

Green soups are visually appealing and if the spices come on right, they will surely appeal to all looking for health food. Go slow on the salt in this soup because it is easy to over salt a spinach preparation.

CHICKEN COCONUT RASAM

INGREDIENTS

500 grams chicken bones
100 grams boneless chicken, cut into
   1 inch cubes
½ cup scraped coconut
3 tablespoons tamarind pulp
2 medium tomatoes, roughly chopped
Salt to taste
2 tablespoons *rasam* powder
8 black peppercorns, crushed

1 teaspoon red chilli powder
½ teaspoon turmeric powder
15 curry leaves
2 tablespoons chopped fresh coriander leaves
2 tablespoons olive oil
1 teaspoon mustard seeds
2-3 whole dried red chillies, broken into two

METHOD

Grind coconut with one cup of warm water. Extract coconut milk and set aside. Reserve the coconut residue. Boil the chicken bones in about six to seven cups of water for fifteen minutes. Skim off the scum from the surface, add tamarind pulp, tomatoes, chicken cubes, salt, *rasam* powder, crushed black peppercorns, red chilli powder, turmeric powder, ten curry leaves and continue cooking. Simmer till the liquid reduces by half and a nice aroma is given out.

Add the drained coconut residue to the *rasam*. Sprinkle coriander leaves and simmer for about three to four minutes. Remove from heat and strain *rasam*. Separate the chicken pieces from the residue and cut into one centimetre cubes and reserve for garnish. Reheat the strained *rasam*, add coconut milk and simmer for a couple of minutes. Remove from heat and add chicken pieces to it. Heat olive oil and temper it with mustard seeds, dry red chillies and remaining curry leaves. Add to the prepared soup and cover immediately to trap the flavours. Serve piping hot. You can squeeze a lemon to make it real tangy.

See page 158 for the recipe of *Rasam* Powder.

ALOO KACHALU CHAAT

INGREDIENTS

2 large potatoes, boiled, cut into 1 inch cubes
1 large sweet potato, boiled, cut into 1 inch cubes
1½ tablespoons lemon juice
Salt to taste
1 inch piece ginger, cut into thin strips
1 large ripe banana
2-3 green pickled olives, sliced
2-3 black pickled olives, sliced
2 tablespoons tamarind pulp
2 green chillies, finely chopped
1 teaspoon *chaat masala*
2 tablespoons chopped fresh coriander leaves

METHOD

Add half a teaspoon of lemon juice and a pinch of salt to ginger strips. Keep in the refrigerator. Peel and cut banana into one inch pieces, apply half a teaspoon of lemon juice and set aside. Place potatoes, sweet potato, banana, green olives and black olives in a mixing bowl. Add remaining lemon juice, tamarind pulp, green chillies, *chaat masala*, salt, coriander leaves and toss lightly. Serve garnished with pickled ginger strips.

See page 159 for the recipe of *Chaat Masala*.

Sweet potatoes have a distinctive sugary flavour, which makes them an excellent addition to *chaats.*

MURGH AUR SHIMLA MIRCH SALAD

INGREDIENTS

2 boneless chicken breasts

1 medium red capsicum, seeded and cut into strips

1 medium green capsicum, seeded and cut into strips

1 medium yellow capsicum, seeded and cut into strips

5-6 green olives

5-6 black olives

For marinade

1 tablespoon olive oil

3 tablespoons yogurt

½ tablespoon green chilli paste

1 teaspoon ginger garlic paste

½ teaspoon *garam masala* powder

5-6 black peppercorns, crushed

Salt to taste

Dressing

4 teaspoons extra virgin olive oil

2 teaspoons lemon juice

2 teaspoons *chaat masala*

Black salt to taste

METHOD

Mix all the ingredients for marinade in a bowl. Add chicken breasts and marinate, preferably in the refrigerator, for an hour. Mix all the ingredients for the dressing and set aside. Grill the chicken breasts in a pre-heated grill, or on a *tawa* (griddle) on medium heat, for eight to ten minutes or until done, turning once or twice, taking care they remain juicy. Allow to cool and cut into one-inch pieces. Add three coloured capsicums, olives and the dressing. Toss lightly and serve immediately.

See page 158 for the recipe of *Garam Masala* Powder.

See page159 for the recipe of *Chaat Masala*.

CARROT, RAISIN AND BLACK OLIVE SALAD

INGREDIENTS

4-5 large carrots
½ cup raisins
6-8 black olives, sliced
2 tablespoons lemon juice
5-6 black peppercorns, crushed
1 green chilli, finely chopped
1 tablespoon honey
Salt to taste
¼ teaspoon black salt
6 walnut kernels, crushed
1 teaspoon extra virgin olive oil
6- 8 fresh mint leaves

METHOD

Thickly grate carrots. Refrigerate till required for use. Combine lemon juice, crushed black peppercorns, green chilli, honey, salt, black salt, walnuts, raisins, black olives and olive oil to make a dressing. Just before serving add the dressing to the grated carrots and toss. Serve garnished with mint leaves.

Low in calories but high in carbohydrates…have a bowlful of this salad when you need perk-me-up food.

TANDOORI MURGH CHAAT

INGREDIENTS

2 boneless chicken breasts, skinned
1 teaspoon Kashmiri red chilli powder
1 teaspoon ginger paste
1 teaspoon garlic paste
½ cup drained yogurt
Salt to taste
1 tablespoon lemon juice
½ teaspoon *garam masala* powder
2½ teaspoons olive oil
1 small green capsicum, seeded and cut into thin strips
½ small red capsicum, seeded and cut into thin strips
½ small yellow capsicum, seeded and cut into thin strips
1 medium onion, sliced
2 green chillies, chopped
2 tablespoons chopped fresh coriander leaves
1 tablespoon lemon juice
1 teaspoon *chaat masala*
½ small unripe green mango, chopped (optional)

METHOD

Make incisions with a sharp knife on the chicken breasts and set aside. Combine Kashmiri red chilli powder, ginger paste, garlic paste, drained yogurt, salt, lemon juice, *garam masala* powder and two teaspoons olive oil well. Apply this mixture to the chicken pieces and leave to marinate for three to four hours preferably in a refrigerator. Preheat oven to 200ºC/400ºF/Gas Mark 6.

Thread the chicken pieces onto skewers and cook in the preheated oven or in a moderately hot *tandoor* (clay oven) for ten to twelve minutes or until almost done. Baste it with the remaining olive oil and cook for another four minutes. When cool, shred chicken pieces and set aside. In a large bowl, combine shredded chicken, green, red and yellow capsicum strips, onion, green chillies, half the coriander leaves, lemon juice, *chaat masala*, unripe mango (if using) and salt and toss to mix well. Transfer onto a serving plate and serve garnished with the remaining coriander leaves.

See page 158 for the recipe of *Garam Masala* Powder.

See page 159 for the recipe of *Chaat Masala*.

Snacks & Starters

TOMATO AND OLIVE UPMA

INGREDIENTS

1 cup semolina

2 medium tomatoes, chopped

10-12 black olives, sliced

½ cup yogurt

Salt to taste

3 tablespoons olive oil

½ teaspoon skinless split black gram

¼ teaspoon mustard seeds

5-6 curry leaves

1 large onion, chopped

½ inch piece ginger, chopped

3-4 green chillies, chopped

2 tablespoons chopped fresh coriander leaves

METHOD

Whisk yogurt with salt and two and half cups of water to make very thin buttermilk. Set aside. Heat olive oil in a *kadai* (wok), add split black gram and mustard seeds and fry for a minute. When the mustard seeds begin to splutter add curry leaves, onion, tomatoes, ginger and green chillies and sauté for a minute. Add *rawa* and continue to sauté on medium heat for four to five minutes till it is lightly coloured and fragrant. Add buttermilk, bring to a boil, reduce heat and continue to cook uncovered, stirring continuously, till all the liquid is absorbed. Adjust seasoning, cover and cook further for two minutes on very low heat. Add black olives and coriander leaves. Stir and cook for a minute. Serve hot.

Upma is the quintessential breakfast in western and southern India. Called variously as *upma*, *uppindi*, *upeet* it all amounts to good use of semolina for a substantial snack. Here I have simply substituted vegetables with olives.

BAIDA ROTI

INGREDIENTS

For the roti

1½ cups refined flour

Salt to taste

1 tablespoon olive oil + to shallow-fry

A pinch of baking powder

1 egg

For the filling

1 cup mutton mince

2 tablespoons olive oil

1 medium onion, grated

2 green chillies, chopped

¼ teaspoon *garam masala* powder

2 tablespoons chopped fresh coriander leaves

8 eggs, whisked

Salt to taste

METHOD

Sift refined flour into a bowl. Add salt, one tablespoon olive oil, baking powder and egg. Mix well and knead into a soft dough adding water as required. Divide the dough into eight equal portions and roll into round balls. Keep the dough covered with a damp cloth. Heat two tablespoons of olive oil in a pan. Add onion and sauté till light brown. Add mutton mince, green chillies and salt. Cover and cook on medium heat for twenty minutes or till the mince is cooked and completely dry.

Add *garam masala* powder and coriander leaves and mix well. Roll out each dough ball into a thin square *chapati*. Place a tablespoon or two of mince in the centre and pour two tablespoons of beaten egg over it. Fold in sides to make a square packet. Heat a non-stick pan and place the *chapati* packet on it. Pour some more beaten egg over and drizzle oil. Slowly turn over and pour a little more of the beaten egg so that the dough-mince packet is covered with egg on all sides. Gently fry on low heat till all the sides are golden and crisp. Cut into half. Serve hot with green chutney.

See page 158 for the recipe of *Garam Masala* Powder.

See page 158 for the recipe of Green Chutney.

PATRA

INGREDIENTS

12 leaves colocasia leaves
1½ cups gram flour
2 teaspoons coriander powder
2 teaspoons roasted cumin powder
1 teaspoon red chilli powder
1 teaspoon turmeric powder
2 teaspoons sesame seeds
½ teaspoon soda bicarbonate
Salt to taste
2 teaspoons green chilli paste

2 teaspoons ginger paste
4 tablespoons olive oil
¼ teaspoon *garam masala* powder
3½ tablespoons grated jaggery
1 lemon sized ball of tamarind
1 teaspoon mustard seeds
A pinch of asafoetida
¼ cup scraped coconut
2 tablespoons chopped fresh coriander leaves

METHOD

Remove the thick stem from the leaves. Wash and gently wipe dry. To make the *masala* take gram flour In a bowl. Mix in coriander powder, roasted cumin powder, red chilli powder and turmeric powder. Add sesame seeds, soda bicarbonate, salt, green chilli paste, ginger paste, two tablespoons olive oil, *garam masala* powder and jaggery. Mix well. Soak the tamarind in a cup of water. Strain the water. Mix in the juice with the *besan* mixture to form a paste. Place a leaf on the worktop, shiny side facing downwards. Apply the *masala* evenly all over.

Place another leaf over it but with its tapering end in the opposite direction of the first one. Apply *masala* over this. Similarly use up three leaves per roll. Fold the sides of the leaves inwards and then start rolling into a tight roll holding from the sides. Tie it up with a string. Similarly make rolls with the remaining leaves and the remaining *masala*. Steam in a steamer for about fifteen to twenty minutes, or till cooked. Remove and set aside to cool. Cut into one-and-a half-inch thick pieces. Heat remaining oil in a *kadai* (wok). Add mustard seeds. When they begin to crackle, add asafoetida and then put in the pieces. Sauté till golden brown. Serve hot, garnished with coconut and coriander leaves.

See page 158 for the recipe of *Garam Masala* Powder.

ALOO KI TIKKI

INGREDIENTS
6 medium potatoes, boiled and mashed
Salt to taste
1 tablespoon olive oil + to deep fry
1 medium onion, chopped
¼ cup grated cottage cheese
¼ cup chopped fresh coriander leaves
6-8 cashew nuts, crushed
½ tablespoon red chilli powder

METHOD
Add salt to mashed potatoes and knead into a smooth dough. Divide into twelve equal portions. Heat one tablespoon of olive oil in a pan and sauté onion till translucent. Cool and mix with *paneer*, coriander leaves, cashew nuts, red chilli powder and salt. Divide the mixture into twelve equal portions. Stuff each portion of mashed potato with a portion of the *paneer* mixture. Roll and shape into *tikkis* (roundels) of approximately two-inch diameter and half-inch thickness. Heat sufficient oil in a *kadai* (wok) and deep-fry the *tikkis* till golden brown. Drain and place on absorbent paper. Serve hot with tomato ketchup or mint chutney.

See page 158 for the recipe of Mint Chutney.

Aloo tikki is perhaps the first thing a new cook will be taught in a *Punjabi* home in stage one. The stuffing, as suggested, comes at stage two! Typically no binding is used in this recipe. However you can add two to three tablespoons of cornflour to the potato mixture. For those who so prefer, shallow-fry the *tikkis* instead of deep-frying.

BESAN METHI CHEELA WITH CHEESE

INGREDIENTS

2 cups gram flour
1 cup chopped fresh fenugreek leaves
2½ cups cottage cheese, grated
1 tablespoon olive oil + to shallow-fry
2 medium onions, chopped
8-10 fresh button mushrooms, sliced
Salt to taste
¼ teaspoon black pepper powder
¼ teaspoon soda bicarbonate
1 teaspoon red chilli powder
1 teaspoon carom seeds
A pinch of asafoetida
2 tablespoons chopped fresh coriander leaves

METHOD

Heat one tablespoon olive oil in a *kadai* (wok) and sauté onions till translucent. Add *methi* and cook for another minute. Add mushrooms and sauté on high heat for a minute. Add salt and black pepper powder. Let cool and mix in cottage cheese. Set aside. In a bowl mix together gram flour, soda bicarbonate, salt, red chilli powder, carom seeds, asafoetida, coriander leaves and sufficient water to make a batter of pouring consistency. Whisk well to ensure there are no lumps. Heat a pan, drizzle a few drops of olive oil, pour a ladle full of batter into the pan and spread it evenly and thinly using the back of the ladle. Cook the *cheela* on both sides using a little more olive oil till golden brown. Place a portion of the stuffing on one side of the *cheela*, fold the other side over it and serve immediately.

The final presentation of this snack belies the simplicity of its preparation. I have it either for breakfast on a rainy day or then as an evening snack when dinner's a little away.

ANGOORI PRAWNS

INGREDIENTS

200 grams prawns/shrimps, shelled and deveined

8-10 black grapes

8-10 red grapes

8-10 green grapes

Salt to taste

A little olive oil to grease

½ cup honey

¾ cup balsamic vinegar

1 teaspoon red chilli flakes

2 tablespoons extra virgin olive oil

METHOD

Skewer the prawns and grapes onto a skewer in the following order: black grape, prawn, red grape and finally green grape. Season with salt and cook on an oiled grill for two to three minutes. Heat a pan and add honey. Add salt and balsamic vinegar and mix well. Add red chilli flakes, mix and set aside. Baste the prawns with extra virgin olive oil and turn around so that they get cooked evenly all round. Once ready, place the prawns and grapes on a platter. Pour the sauce over and serve hot.

Snacks & Starters

TANDOORI CHICKEN

INGREDIENTS

1 whole (800 grams) chicken
2 teaspoons Kashmiri red chilli powder
3 tablespoons lemon juice
Salt to taste
1 cup yogurt
2 tablespoons ginger paste
2 tablespoons garlic paste
½ teaspoon *garam masala* powder
2 tablespoons olive oil + to baste
½ teaspoon *chaat masala*
Onion rings and lemon wedges, to garnish

METHOD

Make incisions with a sharp knife on the chicken breast, legs and thighs. Apply a mixture of one teaspoon Kashmiri red chilli powder, one tablespoon lemon juice and salt over the chicken and set aside for half an hour. For the marinade, tie up yogurt in a piece of muslin and hang over a bowl for fifteen to twenty minutes. Remove the thick yogurt into a bowl. Add the remaining Kashmiri red chilli powder, salt, ginger paste, garlic paste, remaining lemon juice, *garam masala* powder and two tablespoons olive oil. Rub this mixture over the chicken and marinate for three to four hours in a refrigerator. Thread the chicken onto a skewer and cook in a moderately hot *tandoor* (clay oven) or in a preheated oven at 200°C/400°F/Gas Mark 6 for ten to twelve minutes, or until almost done. Baste chicken with a little oil and cook for another four minutes. Remove and set aside. Sprinkle *chaat masala* powder and serve with onion rings and lemon wedges.

See page 158 for the recipe of *Garam Masala* Powder.
See page 159 for the recipe of *Chaat Masala*.

Tandoori chicken is perhaps the best known Indian dish globally. This recipe can make good Chicken *Tikka* too. All you have to do is use boneless chicken pieces instead of whole chicken.

BHAJNEE THALIPEETH
Mixed Flour Bread

INGREDIENTS

3 cups *bhajnee* flour
Salt to taste
½ teaspoon turmeric powder
1 medium onion, finely chopped
2 teaspoons olive oil + to shallow-fry

METHOD

Mix salt, turmeric powder, onion and two teaspoons of olive oil with *bhajnee* flour. Add water as required, a little at a time and form into a soft dough. Divide dough into eight equal portions. Flatten each portion, on a moist banana leaf or a thick polythene sheet, into quarter inch thick discs of four to five inches diameter. Make a hole in the centre of each *thalipeeth*. Heat a *tawa* (griddle), spoon a little oil and transfer *thalipeeth* carefully onto the *tawa*. Spoon a little oil on the sides of *thalipeeth* and cook on low heat for one minute. Turn the *thalipeeth* and cook the other side for one minute or till crisp and golden brown. Serve hot with yogurt.

The only effort in this lies in the making of *bhajnee* flour from scratch. To do that, dry-roast 1 cup wholewheat, 1 cup rice, 2 cups sorghum, 2 cups millet, ¾ cup whole black Bengal gram, ¾ cup skinless split black gram, ½ cup coriander seeds separately. Cool, mix and grind to a fine powder. It can be stored up to one month.

HARA BHARA KABAB

INGREDIENTS

100 grams fresh spinach leaves, blanched and chopped
¾ cup shelled green peas, boiled and mashed
3-4 medium potatoes, boiled and grated
2 green chillies, chopped
2 tablespoons chopped fresh coriander leaves
1 inch piece ginger, chopped
1 teaspoon *chaat masala*
Salt to taste
2 tablespoons cornflour
Olive oil to deep-fry

METHOD

Mix spinach, peas and potatoes. Add green chillies, coriander leaves, ginger, *chaat masala* and salt. Add cornflour for binding. Divide the mixture into twenty-four portions. Shape each portion into a ball and then press it between your palms to give it a flat *tikki* (roundel) shape. Heat sufficient olive oil in a *kadai* (wok). Deep-fry the *tikkis* in hot oil for three to four minutes. Drain and place on an absorbent paper and serve hot.

See page 159 for the recipe of *Chaat Masala*.

Hara Bhara Kabab is one of my favourite recipes as it goes a long way back. I would recommend that you do not use colour in this recipe. If you wish you may increase the quantity of spinach leaves to give a darker green colour. In that case add a little more cornflour for binding. You may also shallow-fry the *Hara Bhara Kabab* on a griddle plate or a *tawa*.

CORN BHEL WITH TOMATO AND OLIVES

INGREDIENTS

1 cup corn niblets, boiled
1 large tomato, finely chopped
8 green olives, pitted and halved
8 black olives, pitted and halved
1 large onion, chopped
2 medium potatoes, boiled and cut into ½ cm cubes
2 teaspoons *chaat masala*
3-4 green chillies, chopped
2 tablespoons green chutney
2 tablespoons sweet date and tamarind chutney
4 tablespoons chopped fresh coriander leaves
1½ teaspoons lemon juice
Salt to taste
Cornflakes, crushed for garnish

METHOD

Mix corn niblets, tomato, onion, potatoes, *chaat masala*, green chillies, green chutney, sweet date and tamarind chutney and coriander leaves well. Add lemon juice, salt and mix. Divide into individual servings, sprinkle olives and crushed cornflakes and serve immediately.

See page 159 for the recipe of *Chaat Masala.*
See page 159 for the recipe of Sweet Date and Tamarind Chutney.
See page 158 for the recipe of Green Chutney.

Recipe courtesy:
Anupa Das

MUTTON SHAAMI KABAB

INGREDIENTS

600 grams boneless mutton, cut into ½ inch pieces
½ cup split Bengal gram, soaked
2 medium onions, chopped
2 tablespoons chopped fresh coriander leaves
2 tablespoons chopped fresh mint leaves
2 teaspoons lemon juice
3 tablespoons olive oil + to shallow fry
½ teaspoon cumin seeds
1 teaspoon coriander seeds
5-6 black peppercorns

3-4 black cardamoms
2 inch piece ginger, chopped
10-12 garlic cloves, chopped
1 teaspoon red chilli powder
1 teaspoon *garam masala* powder
½ teaspoon mace and green cardamom powder
Salt to taste

To serve
2 medium onions, cut into fine rings
Fresh mint chutney as required

METHOD

Mix onions, coriander and mint leaves with lemon juice to make a stuffing. Divide into sixteen equal portions and set aside. Heat two tablespoons of olive oil in a pressure cooker and add cumin seeds, coriander seeds, black peppercorns and black cardamoms and stir-fry for half a minute on medium heat. Add ginger, garlic and red chilli powder. Add boneless mutton pieces and *chana dal*. Add two cups of water and bring to a boil. Put the lid on and cook under pressure till six whistles are given out. This may take about twenty five minutes. Open the lid when the pressure has reduced. Cook on high heat to dry out the mixture completely, stirring continuously. Remove from heat and cool.

Grind mutton and *chana dal* mixture to a smooth consistency. Add *garam masala* powder, mace and green cardamom powder and salt. Mix well and check the seasoning. Divide into sixteen equal portions. Flatten one portion in the palm of your hand and place a portion of onion stuffing in the centre. Shape into roundel and flatten slightly. Similarly shape the rest of the mutton mixture and stuffing. Heat sufficient oil in a frying pan and shallow fry the *kababs* till golden. Drain and place on an absorbent paper. Serve hot with onion rings and mint *chutney*.

See page 158 for the recipe of *Garam Masala* Powder.

See page 158 for the recipe of Mint Chutney.

PRAWN VARUVAL
Crisp Fried Prawns

INGREDIENTS

12-16 medium prawns, shelled and deveined
1 inch piece ginger
6-8 garlic cloves
1 teaspoon roasted cumin powder
1 tablespoon tamarind pulp
2 teaspoons red chilli powder
½ teaspoon turmeric powder
2 tablespoons rice flour
Salt to taste
¼ cup olive oil
1 tablespoon lemon juice

METHOD

Grind ginger and garlic to a fine paste. Mix ginger-garlic paste with roasted cumin powder, tamarind pulp, red chilli powder, turmeric powder, rice flour, salt and two tablespoons olive oil. Marinate prawns in this mixture and set aside for at least two hours, preferably in the refrigerator. Heat remaining oil in a pan, add the marinated prawns and cook for a minute on high heat. Turn over the prawns and cook for another minute. Reduce heat and cook for two to three minutes turning the prawns occasionally for uniform cooking. Drain and place on an absorbent paper. Sprinkle lemon juice and serve hot.

Ideal dish for those who want to be initiated into the art of non-vegetarian cookery. Simple to make, great to taste, it is ideally accompanied with rice and *rasam*. They can be served as starters with cocktails too.

KHAAS SEEKH

INGREDIENTS

1 cup cottage cheese, grated
600 grams chicken mince
1½ teaspoons green cardamom powder
1 tablespoon *garam masala* powder
1 tablespoon chopped fresh mint leaves
1 egg
Salt to taste
1 teaspoon white pepper powder
Olive oil to baste
1 teaspoon *chaat masala*
Satay sticks

For Chopped Chutney

2 tablespoons chopped fresh coriander leaves
2 tablespoons chopped fresh mint leaves
2 spring onions with greens, chopped
2 green chillies, seeded and chopped
½ inch piece ginger, minced
3 garlic cloves, minced
Salt to taste
1 tablespoon lemon juice

METHOD

Soak the satay sticks in water for a while. Preheat oven to 220°C/425°F/Gas Mark 7. Take *paneer* in a bowl. Add half the green cardamom powder, half the *garam masala* powder, mint leaves and mix, mashing with your hands. Take a portion of this mixture and place on a satay stick and press it around the stick till it is a thin layer. Press the ends firmly. Take chicken *keema* in another bowl. Break an egg and add. Add salt, remaining green cardamom powder, white pepper powder and remaining *garam masala* powder and mix well. Take a portion of this mixture and spread it over the *paneer* mixture. Similarly prepare the other *seekhs*. You can keep the *seekhs* in the refrigerator for some time before cooking.

Meanwhile, mix all the ingredients for the Chopped Chutney and set aside. Bake *seekhs* in the pre-heated oven for ten to fifteen minutes or till done and golden on the surface, basting with a little olive oil in between. Alternatively grill on a *tawa* (griddle) drizzling olive oil all around as they cook. Serve hot sprinkled with *chaat masala* accompanied with Chopped Chutney.

See page 158 for the recipe of *Garam Masala* Powder.

See page 159 for the recipe of *Chaat Masala*.

Khaas seekh is *khaas,* meaning special. Besides it makes a well presented tempting starter. I especially love this for two reasons: it is simple to prepare and is loaded with nutrition.

PALAK PANEER

INGREDIENTS

900 grams (2 large bunches) fresh spinach leaves
200 grams cottage cheese, cut into ½ inch cubes
2-3 green chillies, chopped
3 tablespoons olive oil
½ teaspoon cumin seeds
8-10 garlic cloves, chopped
Salt to taste
1 tablespoon lemon juice
4 tablespoons cream

METHOD

Remove stems, wash spinach thoroughly in running water. Blanch in salted boiling water for two minutes. Refresh in chilled water. Squeeze out excess water. Grind spinach into a fine paste along with green chillies. Heat olive oil in a pan. Add cumin seeds. When they begin to change colour, add garlic and sauté for half a minute. Add the spinach purée and stir. Check seasoning. Add water if required. When the gravy comes to a boil, add the cottage cheese and mix well. Stir in lemon juice. Finally add cream. Serve hot.

ALUCHI PATAL BHAJI
Colocasia in Sour Gravy

INGREDIENTS

8 colocasia leaves, shredded
¼ cup split Bengal gram, soaked
Salt to taste
3 tablespoons tamarind pulp
3 tablespoons olive oil
½ teaspoon mustard seeds
5-6 curry leaves
A generous pinch of asafoetida
¼ teaspoon fenugreek seeds
4 garlic cloves, finely chopped
4-5 green chillies, finely chopped
¼ teaspoon turmeric powder
3 tablespoons gram flour
¼ cup raw peanuts
1 tablespoon grated jaggery
½ cup scraped coconut

METHOD

Boil *arbi* leaves with salt, one and a half tablespoons of tamarind pulp and *chana dal* in four cups of water till done. Heat olive oil in a pan. Add mustard seeds, curry leaves, asafoetida, fenugreek seeds, garlic and sauté for one minute. Add green chillies, turmeric powder and sauté for half a minute. Add *besan*, mix and sauté for a minute. Add the boiled mixture and half a cup of water if required. Adjust salt and stir. Add raw peanuts and adjust water. Cook for five minutes and add grated jaggery. Bring to a boil again and add the remaining tamarind pulp and mix. Add coconut and some more water if required and cook on medium heat for half an hour, stirring occasionally. Serve hot.

Main Course

ALOO POSTO

INGREDIENTS

5-6 medium potatoes, cut into 1 inch cubes
4 tablespoons poppy seeds
2 tablespoons olive oil
½ teaspoon onion seeds
Salt to taste
½ teaspoon sugar
2 green chillies

METHOD

Soak poppy seeds in one cup of warm water for fifteen to twenty minutes. Drain and grind to a fine paste. Heat olive oil in a pan. Add *kalonji* and stir-fry briefly. Add potato pieces and cook on medium heat for five minutes, stirring frequently. Add poppy seed paste, stir and add half a cup of water. Cover and cook on low heat till the potatoes are almost done. Uncover, add salt, sugar and slit green chillies. Continue to cook for a minute more or till potatoes are completely cooked and serve hot.

Bengalis use a lot of nutritious seeds in their cooking. This particular dish is focussed on poppy seeds. I suggest you try this recipe at a Sunday lunch as the slumberous effect of poppy seeds will warrant a nap. Traditionally mustard oil is used as the cooking medium but I have adapted the recipe to make a grand entry in this collection.

CHORCHORI

INGREDIENTS

¼ medium cauliflower, small florets
2 medium potatoes, cut into ½ inch cubes
1 medium sweet potato, cut into ½ inch cubes
100 grams red pumpkin, cut into ½ inch cubes
1 medium brinjal, cut into ½ inch cubes
6-8 French beans, cut into ½ inch pieces
6-8 fresh spinach leaves, shredded
1½ tablespoons olive oil
1½ teaspoons *paanch phoron*
½ teaspoon red chilli powder
¼ teaspoon turmeric powder
Salt to taste
2 green chillies, slit
½ teaspoon sugar

METHOD

Heat olive oil in a pan. Add *paanch phoron* and when it starts spluttering, add red chilli powder, stir briefly and add the prepared vegetables. Stir and add turmeric powder, slit green chillies, sugar and salt to taste. Reduce heat, cover and cook for eight to ten minutes, stirring occasionally or till potato pieces are cooked till *chorchori* is dry. Serve hot.

Note: *Paanch Phoron* is a mixture of equal quantities of mustard seeds, cumin seeds, fenugreek seeds, fennel seeds and onion seeds.

There is a story behind this mixed vegetable dish. In many Bengali households, shopping for fresh vegetables was the duty of the man of the house. And it was done once a week on his day off from work. By the end of the week, the lady of the house was left with bits of all the various vegetables. Hence this innovation! Mind you, a delicious and nutritious one!

MIRCHI KA SALAN

INGREDIENTS

18-20 big green chillies
2 tablespoons olive oil + to deep fry
2 tablespoons sesame seeds
1 tablespoon coriander seeds
1 teaspoon cumin seeds
½ cup roasted peanuts
2 whole dried chillies
1 inch ginger, roughly chopped
6-8 garlic cloves
1 teaspoon mustard seeds
8-10 curry leaves
1 medium onion, grated
1 teaspoon turmeric powder
2 tablespoons tamarind pulp
Salt to taste

METHOD

Wash, wipe and slit green chillies lengthways without cutting the chillies into two. Heat sufficient olive oil in a *kadai* (wok) and deep-fry for one minute. Drain and place on absorbent paper and set aside. To make *masala* paste, dry-roast sesame seeds, coriander seeds and cumin seeds. Cool and grind them to a paste along with peanuts, whole dried red chillies, ginger and garlic.

Heat two tablespoons of olive oil in a pan, add mustard seeds, let them splutter and add curry leaves. Sauté for half a minute and add onion. Sauté, stirring continuously, till onion is light golden brown. Add turmeric powder and mix well. Add *masala* paste and cook for three minutes, stirring constantly. Stir in one and half cups of water and bring it to a boil. Reduce the heat and cook for ten minutes. Add tamarind pulp (dissolved in half a cup of water, if it is too thick). Add fried green chillies and salt and cook on low heat for eight to ten minutes. Serve hot.

In Hyderabad, *Mirchi ka Salan* is traditionally served as an accompaniment to *biryanis*. Some people like to add grated coconut to the *masala* paste, but I prefer *Mirchi ka Salan* without coconut. This gravy is referred to as *Tili* (*Til*-Sesame) *aur Falli* (*Moongfalli* - Peanuts) gravy.

KER SANGRI
Dried Beans and Berries

INGREDIENTS

½ cup berries
1 cup dried beans
1 cup + 4 teaspoons yogurt
4 tablespoons olive oil
1 teaspoon cumin seeds
5-6 whole dried red chillies, broken into two
1 teaspoon garlic paste
1 teaspoon ginger paste
½ teaspoon turmeric powder
1 teaspoon red chilli powder
1 teaspoon coriander powder
5-6 dried pieces of mango
Salt to taste
1 teaspoon dried mango powder
1 tablespoon chopped fresh coriander leaves
1 tablespoon chopped and fried garlic

METHOD

Soak berries and dried beans in one cup of beaten yogurt overnight. Take them out of the yogurt and wash under running water. Boil them for fifteen to twenty minutes in two cups of water with salt. Drain. Heat olive oil in a *kadai* (wok). Add cumin seeds, broken red chillies, garlic paste and ginger paste and sauté. Add a little water, turmeric powder, red chilli powder and coriander powder and mix. Add dried mango pieces and four teaspoons of yogurt and mix. Add *ker* and *sangri* to the *masala* and mix. Add salt, *amchur* and coriander leaves. Mix well. Serve garnished with fried garlic.

DAHI BAINGAN

INGREDIENTS

6-8 medium brinjals, long variety
2 cups yogurt
Salt to taste
2 tablespoons olive oil + to deep fry
¼ teaspoon asafoetida

3-4 green cardamoms
1 tablespoon fennel powder
½ tablespoon dried ginger powder
2 teaspoons *Kashmiri* red chilli powder

METHOD

Wash and cut brinjals into quarters lengthways and keep in water till further use. Whisk yogurt and salt together. Heat sufficient olive oil in a *kadai* (wok). Drain, pat dry and deep-fry brinjals till light brown. Drain and place on an absorbent paper. Heat two tablespoons olive oil in a pan. Add asafoetida and green cardamoms. Stir-fry briefly and immediately add the whisked yogurt. Stir in fennel powder, dried ginger powder and *Kashmiri* red chilli powder. Cook on medium heat for two to three minutes and add fried brinjals. Reduce heat and cook covered for three to four minutes. Adjust seasoning and serve hot.

Eggplants are one of the most popular vegetables in India, and the techniques and ingredients used in their preparation change from region to region, household to household. *Kashmiris* use a lot of fennel and dried ginger in their food. In this recipe I find that the two add that special touch to this most popular vegetable.

UNDHIYO

INGREDIENTS

25-30 broad beans, cut into 1 inch pieces
6-8 small potatoes, diced
100 grams yam, diced
2 unripe bananas, diced
3-4 small brinjals
2 inch piece ginger
6-8 garlic cloves
4 green chillies
3 tablespoons chopped fresh coriander leaves
5 tablespoons olive oil + to deep fry
A pinch of asafoetida
1 teaspoon mustard seeds
Salt to taste
1 teaspoon turmeric powder
½ cup scraped coconut
For *muthiya* (fried dumplings)
¼ cup gram flour
½ cup chopped fresh fenugreek leaves
½ inch piece ginger, grated
1-2 green chillies, chopped
Salt to taste

METHOD

Make a paste of ginger, garlic and green chillies. Add coriander leaves and mix. To make *muthiyas*, mix all the *muthiya* ingredients and prepare a stiff dough. Divide into small portions and shape each into one-inch long and half-inch thick rolls. Heat sufficient olive oil in a *kadai* (wok) and deep-fry *muthiyas* till crisp and golden brown. Drain and place on an absorbent paper and set aside.

Heat five tablespoons olive oil in a thick-bottomed *handi* (a thick-bottomed vessel), add asafoetida and mustard seeds. When mustard seeds crackle, add ginger-garlic-green chilli paste and broad beans. Place the rest of the vegetables in layers one on top of the other. Sprinkle salt to taste and turmeric powder. Cook for five minutes on high heat. Pour one cup of water, cover and simmer on very low heat for ten to fifteen minutes. Add fried *muthiyas* and continue to cook for fifteen minutes. Toss the vegetables occasionally but do not use a spoon to stir. Serve hot garnished with coconut.

PINDI CHHOLAY

INGREDIENTS

1½ cups chickpeas, soaked overnight
1 tablespoon tea leaves
2 inch piece ginger
8-10 garlic cloves
Salt to taste
2 tablespoons coriander powder
2 tablespoons cumin powder
1½ teaspoons red chilli powder
½ teaspoon turmeric powder
½ teaspoon dried mango powder
2 tablespoons cumin seeds
1 tablespoon pomegranate seeds
½ cup olive oil
4-6 green chillies, slit
2 medium tomatoes, quartered
1 teaspoon *garam masala* powder

METHOD

Tie tea leaves in a piece of muslin to form a bundle. Grind ginger and garlic to a fine paste. Drain chickpeas and put them in a pressure cooker. Add six to eight cups water, salt and tea leaves bundle and pressure cook for four to five whistles or twenty minutes or until soft and completely cooked. Drain the chickpeas and reserve the cooking liquor. Mix together coriander powder, cumin powder, red chilli powder, turmeric powder and *amchur*. Dry-roast cumin till they turn dark brown. Dry-roast *anardana* and grind to a powder along with roasted cumin seeds.

Heat four tablespoons of olive oil in a *kadai* (wok). Add green chillies and ginger-garlic paste. Stir-fry briefly. Add the mixed spice powder and stir-fry for half a minute. Stir in half cup of the reserved cooking liquor and cook for two minutes. Add the cooked chickpeas, salt to taste, one cup of reserved cooking liquor and cook on high heat for three to four minutes, stirring occasionally. Top it with tomatoes, sprinkle *garam masala* powder, roasted *anardana*-cumin powder. Heat the remaining oil and pour over the prepared chickpeas. Stir well, adjust seasoning and serve hot.

See page 158 for the recipe of *Garam Masala* Powder

GOBHI MATAR

INGREDIENTS

1 medium cauliflower, separated into florets
1 cup shelled green peas
2 tablespoons olive oil
1 teaspoon cumin seeds
1 teaspoon ginger paste
1 teaspoon garlic paste
2 teaspoons coriander powder
½ teaspoon red chilli powder
½ teaspoon turmeric powder
¼ cup tomato purée
Salt to taste
1 teaspoon *garam masala* powder
½ teaspoon dried mango powder
1 green chilli, slit
1 tablespoon chopped fresh coriander leaves

METHOD

Heat olive oil in a *kadai* (wok) and add cumin seeds. When they begin to change colour add ginger paste and garlic paste. Sauté for half a minute. Add coriander powder, red chilli powder and turmeric powder. Sauté for another half a minute. Add cauliflower florets, green peas, half a cup of water and tomato purée. Add salt and mix. Cover and cook for eight to ten minutes, stirring occasionally. Add *garam masala* powder and *amchur* and mix. Garnish with green chilli and coriander leaves and serve hot.

See page 158 for the recipe of *Garam Masala* Powder.

This transports me to my childhood. Winter afternoons, back from school, hot *Gobhi Matar* with thick *paranthas* and fresh *dahi* (yogurt). We used to bask in the sun till it went down....

CHANA AND JACKFRUIT SUKKE

INGREDIENTS

1 cup Bengal gram
½ kilogram jackfruit
3 tablespoons olive oil
Salt to taste
½ teaspoon mustard seeds
1 sprig curry leaves
A pinch asafoetida
1 tablespoon grated jaggery

For paste

1 teaspoon coriander seeds
½ teaspoon skinless split black gram
¼ teaspoon fenugreek seeds
3-4 whole dried red chillies, broken
1 cup scraped coconut
1 tablespoon tamarind pulp

METHOD

Soak *chana* in three cups of water for three to four hours. Drain. Apply a little olive oil to your palms and knife and remove skin of jackfruit. Further cut the jackfruit into two centimetres pieces. Apply salt and set aside. Steam the pieces in a steamer for five minutes. Remove from steamer and set aside. Pressure cook soaked *chana* in two cups of water for about three whistles or till soft. Heat one teaspoon of olive oil in a *kadai* (wok).

Add coriander seeds, split black gram and fenugreek seeds. Sauté till lightly browned. Add broken red chillies and sauté for a minute. Grind to a coarse *masala* paste along with coconut, tamarind pulp and sufficient water. Heat remaining olive oil in a *kadai*. Add mustard seeds and curry leaves and let the mustard seeds splutter. Add asafoetida and the ground *masala*. Stir well and cook for two minutes. Add boiled *chana* and stir well. Add steamed jackfruit pieces, salt and jaggery. Stir, add half a cup of water and cook for five minutes on low heat stirring occasionally. Remove from heat and serve hot.

BAGHARE BAINGAN

INGREDIENTS

250 grams small brinjals
2 medium onions, quartered
1½ teaspoons coriander seeds
1½ tablespoons sesame seeds
2 tablespoons peanuts
½ teaspoon cumin seeds
¾ teaspoon poppy seeds
1 tablespoon grated dried coconut
A pinch of fenugreek seeds
1 inch ginger, roughly chopped
6-8 garlic cloves, roughly chopped
Salt to taste
A pinch of turmeric power
½ teaspoon red chilli powder
½ teaspoon grated jaggery or sugar
2 tablespoons tamarind pulp
½ cup olive oil
1 sprig curry leaves

METHOD

Wash brinjals and make slits along the length taking care that the brinjal is held together at the stem. Dry-roast onions on a *tawa* (griddle) till they turn lightly brown and soften. Dry-roast together coriander seeds, sesame seeds, peanuts, cumin seeds, poppy seeds, dried coconut and fenugreek seeds till they begin to change colour and give out a nice aroma. Grind together roasted onions, roasted spices, ginger, garlic, salt, turmeric powder, red chilli powder and jaggery or sugar to a very fine paste. Add tamarind pulp and mix well.

Stuff this *masala* into the slit brinjals and reserve the remaining. Heat olive oil in a *kadai* (wok), add curry leaves and sauté for a minute. Add the stuffed brinjals and sauté for about ten minutes. Add the reserved *masala* and mix gently. Add two cups of water, cover and cook over low heat till the brinjals are fully cooked and oil comes to the surface. Serve hot.

PANEER KEEMA

INGREDIENTS

250 grams cottage cheese, crumbled
2 tablespoons olive oil
1 large onion, chopped
1 teaspoon cumin seeds
1 teaspoon red chilli powder
1 green chilli, finely chopped
Salt to taste
½ teaspoon *garam masala* powder
1 tablespoon chopped fresh coriander leaves

METHOD

Heat olive oil in a *kadai*. Add cumin seeds. As they begin to change colour add onion and sauté till lightly browned. Add red chilli powder. Sauté for thirty seconds. Add *paneer,* green chilli, salt and *garam masala* powder. Sauté for half a minute. Garnish with coriander leaves and serve hot.

See page 158 for the recipe of *Garam Masala* Powder.

Ideal for a relaxed breakfast or brunch I like this simple dish because it is quick fix. Just roll it up in *chapatis* and enjoy!

TENDER COCONUT AND CASHEW NUT SUKKE

INGREDIENTS

1 cup tender coconut flesh, cut into 2 inch x ¼ inch slices
25-30 cashew nuts, soaked for 1 hour
2 tablespoons scraped coconut
1 tablespoon olive oil
½ teaspoon cumin seeds
3-4 garlic cloves, crushed
1 large onion, chopped
5-6 curry leaves
2 medium tomatoes, chopped
½ teaspoon turmeric powder
1 teaspoon red chilli powder
Sea salt to taste
3 tablespoons tomato purée
½ cup thick coconut milk (see below)
2 tablespoons chopped fresh coriander leaves

METHOD

Heat olive oil in a pan and add cumin seeds, garlic and onions. Sauté till lightly browned. Add curry leaves and stir. Add tomatoes, turmeric powder, red chilli powder and cook for a while. Add the soaked cashew nuts and a little water. Cook for a while, then add sea salt, tomato purée and mix. Add coconut slices and scraped coconut and stir. Add coconut milk and cook till almost dry. Add chopped coriander leaves and mix well. Serve hot.

Note: To make coconut milk, first scrape coconut. Put it in a blender. For each cup of scraped coconut, use one-fourth cup of warm water and blend it properly. Pass it through a piece of muslin/strainer pressing firmly to extract all the juice (first milk). This process can be repeated to get the second and thinner milk from the same solids.

FISH AMBOTIK
Hot & Sour Pomfret

INGREDIENTS

2 medium pomfrets (400 grams each), cut into ½ inch thick slices
Salt to taste
1 teaspoon turmeric powder
1 tablespoon coriander seeds
1 teaspoon cumin seeds
1 cup scraped coconut
8-10 whole dry red chillies
1 inch piece ginger, chopped
8-10 garlic cloves, chopped
5 cloves
2 inch stick cinnamon
1½ tablespoons vinegar
3 tablespoons olive oil
2 medium onions, chopped
4-5 green chillies, slit
1½ tablespoons tamarind pulp

METHOD

Marinate the fish with salt and turmeric powder. Dry-roast coriander seeds and cumin seeds. To make the *masala,* grind coconut, whole red chillies, coriander seeds, cumin seeds, ginger, garlic, cloves, cinnamon and vinegar to a very fine paste with a little water. Heat olive oil in a pan. Add onion and sauté till golden brown. Add ground *masala* and cook on high heat for two minutes stirring continuously. Add three cups of water and bring the gravy to a boil. Add green chillies and stir. Add the marinated fish pieces and simmer for five minutes. Add tamarind pulp and adjust salt. Stir gently and cook on low heat for five minutes. Serve hot with steamed rice.

Recipe courtesy:
Neena Murdeshwar

CHICKEN CHETTINAAD

INGREDIENTS

1 kilogram chicken, 12 pieces
6-8 whole dried red chillies
½ coconut, scraped
2 teaspoons poppy seeds
1 teaspoon coriander seeds
½ teaspoon cumin seeds
3 green cardamoms
2 cloves
1 inch stick cinnamon
½ star anise
1 teaspoon fennel seeds
2 inch piece ginger, roughly chopped
10-12 garlic cloves
½ cup olive oil
1 large onion, chopped
10-12 curry leaves
3 medium tomatoes, chopped
1 teaspoon red chilli powder
½ teaspoon turmeric powder
Juice of 1 lemon
2 tablespoons chopped fresh coriander leaves
Salt to taste

METHOD

Roast dried red chillies, coconut, poppy seeds, coriander seeds, cumin seeds, green cardamom, cloves, cinnamon, star anise, fennel seeds in two tablespoons of olive oil and grind to a paste along with ginger and garlic. Heat remaining olive oil in a *degchi* (a wide thick-bottomed vessel) and fry onion till golden. Add curry leaves and the ground paste and sauté for some time. Add tomatoes, red chilli powder, turmeric powder and salt to taste. Add chicken and mix. Cook for five minutes and then add two cups of water, lemon juice, cover and cook till the chicken is done. Serve hot garnished with coriander leaves and accompanied with boiled rice or *parantha* (type of Indian bread).

SAAGWALA GOSHT

INGREDIENTS

600 grams mutton, cut into 1½ inch pieces on bone
500 grams fresh spinach leaves
Salt to taste
5 green chillies
4 tablespoons olive oil
2 bay leaves
4 cloves
1 inch stick cinnamon
6 green cardamoms
2 black cardamoms
1 teaspoon cumin seeds
3 medium onions, sliced
6-8 garlic cloves, chopped
1 tablespoon ginger paste
1 tablespoon garlic paste
1 teaspoon red chilli powder
1 inch piece ginger, cut into thin strips

METHOD

Blanch spinach leaves in salted boiling water for one minute. Drain well and coarsely grind it along with green chillies. Heat olive oil in a thick-bottomed pan. Add bay leaves, cloves, cinnamon, green cardamoms, black cardamoms and cumin seeds. When cumin seeds begin to change colour, add onions. Cook till onions are translucent. Add chopped garlic and mix well. Add ginger paste, garlic paste, red chilli powder and mutton pieces. Cook on high heat, stirring continuously. Add three cups of water and cook covered , on medium heat, for thirty to thirty five minutes or until mutton is almost done. Add salt and spinach and cook till mutton is fully blended with spinach and is tender. Serve hot, garnished with ginger strips.

KAIRI MURGH

INGREDIENTS

1 kilogram chicken, cut into 1½ inch pieces
2 medium unripe mangoes
½ tablespoon ginger paste
½ tablespoon garlic paste
Salt to taste
2 teaspoons *garam masala* powder
½ tablespoon green chilli paste
4-5 cloves
3 tablespoons olive oil
2 medium onions, sliced
¼ teaspoon turmeric powder
1½ teaspoons red chilli powder
2 teaspoons coriander powder
2 tablespoons chopped fresh coriander leaves

METHOD

Peel and cut unripe mangoes into small pieces. Purée half of the pieces. In a bowl, marinate chicken with half the ginger paste, half the garlic paste, salt, half the *garam masala* powder, half the green chilli paste, puréed mango for about an hour, preferably in the refrigerator. Place a coal over the gas flame and when it is red hot put it in a *katori* (small metal bowl) and place in the centre of the marinated chicken. Place a few cloves over the coal and pour one tablespoon of olive oil on it and immediately cover it with a lid. Let it stand for a few minutes. Heat the remaining olive oil in a *kadai* (wok), add onions and sauté till translucent. Add the remaining ginger paste, garlic paste, green chilli paste and sauté for two minutes.

Add marinated chicken, turmeric powder, red chilli powder, coriander powder, remaining *garam masala* powder and unripe mango pieces. Stir so that the *masala* coats all the chicken pieces evenly. Cook on high heat for three to four minutes. Adjust salt, add coriander leaves and a little water. Cover and cook for ten to twelve minutes or till done. Serve hot.

See page 158 for the recipe of *Garam Masala* Powder.

KOZHI VARTHA KARI
Pepper & Coconut Chicken

INGREDIENTS

1 kilogram chicken, cut into 16 pieces
2 whole dried red chillies
2 inch piece ginger
6-8 garlic cloves
1 teaspoon red chilli powder
1 tablespoon lemon juice
1 teaspoon turmeric powder
Salt to taste
5 tablespoons olive oil
2 medium onions, chopped
12-15 curry leaves
3 medium tomatoes, chopped
2 teaspoons coriander powder
1 tablespoon tamarind pulp
1 teaspoon *garam masala* powder
16-18 black peppercorns, coarsely crushed
2 tablespoons chopped fresh coriander leaves

METHOD

Make a paste of dried red chillies, ginger and garlic. Marinate the chicken pieces in chilli-ginger-garlic paste, red chilli powder, lemon juice, turmeric powder and salt for three hours preferably in the refrigerator. Heat three tablespoons of olive oil in a thick-bottomed pan and sauté the marinated chicken on high heat for four to five minutes or till chicken pieces are dry and a little browned.

Take out chicken pieces and set aside. Add the remaining oil in the pan and fry onions till brown. Add curry leaves and stir well. Add tomatoes, salt and coriander powder and cook till oil separates from the *masala*. Add the chicken and a little water. Cover and cook on medium heat for five minutes or till the chicken is done and the *masala* coats the pieces. Add tamarind pulp dissolved in half cup of water. Add *garam masala* powder. Simmer for ten minutes, stirring occasionally. Adjust the seasoning and add crushed black peppercorns. Garnish with coriander leaves and serve hot.

See page 158 for the recipe of *Garam Masala* Powder.

SHAHI KORMA

INGREDIENTS
600 grams boneless mutton, cut into 1 inch cubes
4 tablespoons olive oil
4-5 green cardamoms
2 inch stick cinnamon
½ blade mace
4-5 cloves
3 medium onions, chopped
1 tablespoon ginger-garlic paste
1 tablespoon coriander powder
1½ teaspoons red chilli powder
Salt to taste
½ cup yogurt, whisked
¼ cup cashew nut paste
¼ teaspoon nutmeg powder
1 teaspoon *garam masala* powder
½ cup fresh cream

METHOD
Heat olive oil in a thick-bottomed pan and add green cardamoms, cinnamon, mace and cloves. When they start to splutter, add onions and sauté till lightly browned. Add ginger-garlic paste and cook for one minute. Stir constantly as the paste may stick to the bottom. Add mutton cubes and cook on a high heat for three to four minutes stirring constantly. Add coriander powder, red chilli powder and salt. Cook for another two to three minutes. Add yogurt and three cups water. When it starts to boil, reduce heat, cover and cook for twenty to twenty five minutes or till the mutton is almost cooked and tender. Add cashew nut paste dissolved in a cup of water. Cook on a high heat for five minutes, stirring continuously. Stir in nutmeg powder and *garam masala* powder. Cook for five more minutes on medium heat. Finish off with fresh cream. Simmer for ten minutes. Serve hot.

See page 158 for the recipe of *Garam Masala* Powder.

ANDHRA MUTTON CURRY

INGREDIENTS

500 grams mutton, cubed
Salt to taste
¼ teaspoon turmeric powder
1 teaspoon poppy seeds
½ teaspoon fennel seeds
4 black peppercorns
1 teaspoon coriander seeds
1 teaspoon cumin seeds
1 inch stick cinnamon
2 cloves
2 green cardamoms
4 tablespoons olive oil
10 curry leaves
3 medium onions, chopped
1 teaspoon ginger-garlic paste
½ teaspoon red chilli powder
2 teaspoons black pepper powder
1 large tomato, chopped
2 tablespoons chopped fresh coriander leaves

METHOD

Pressure cook mutton pieces with two cups of water, salt and turmeric powder for six whistles. Open the lid when the pressure reduces, drain and reserve the cooking liquor. Dry-roast poppy seeds, fennel seeds, black peppercorns, coriander seeds, cumin seeds, cinnamon, cloves and green cardamoms. Cool and grind to a fine powder. Heat olive oil in *kadai* (wok). Add curry leaves and onions. Sauté till the onions are brown. Add ginger-garlic paste, red chilli powder and half the black pepper powder and sauté for a minute. Add tomato and mutton pieces, cook on high heat till the tomato is soft. Add salt and the spice powder and simmer for five minutes. Add the reserved cooking liquor and one cup of water and bring to a boil. Simmer till all the mutton pieces get well coated with thick gravy. Add the remaining black pepper powder and stir well. Garnish with coriander leaves and serve hot.

GONGURA CHICKEN

INGREDIENTS

800 grams whole chicken, 8 pieces
20-25 roselle leaves, chopped
10 garlic cloves
½ inch piece ginger
6 tablespoons poppy seeds
4 tablespoons olive oil
5 green chillies, broken into 2 pieces
1 teaspoon cumin seeds
 4 medium onions, chopped
1 teaspoons red chilli powder
1½ teaspoons *garam masala* powder
2 teaspoons coriander seeds, roasted and crushed
Salt to taste
2 tablespoons chopped fresh coriander leaves

METHOD

Grind half the garlic with ginger into a fine paste. Chop the remaining garlic cloves. Soak poppy seeds in one-fourth cup of water for half an hour and then grind into a fine paste. Heat two tablespoons of olive oil in a pan and stir-fry chopped garlic, *gongura* leaves and green chillies. Set aside.

Heat remaining olive oil in another pan, add cumin seeds, sauté till they change colour. Add onions and sauté till golden brown. Add ginger and garlic paste. Sauté for a minute. Add red chilli powder, poppy seeds paste, *garam masala* powder and crushed coriander seeds. Add chicken and sauté for three to four minutes. Add two cups of water and salt. Cook covered for five minutes. Add the *gongura* leaves fried with garlic and green chillies. Stir and cook, uncovered, for another ten to twelve minutes or till the chicken is cooked. Serve hot garnished with coriander leaves.

See page 158 for the recipe of *Garam Masala* Powder.

MALABAR CHEMEEN KARI

INGREDIENTS

25-30 small prawns, shelled and deveined
1 teaspoon turmeric powder
Salt to taste
2 cups scraped coconut
6 tablespoons olive oil
9-10 shallots chopped
1 tablespoon red chilli powder
1 tablespoon coriander powder
6 green chillies, slit
4-6 curd chillies, slit
2 sprigs curry leaves
6 pieces *kodumpulli* (fish tamarind)
1 teaspoon fenugreek seeds, lightly pounded
4 whole dried red chillies
2 drumsticks, remove string, cut into 1 inch pieces
1 medium unripe mango, cut into wedges

METHOD

Marinate prawns in half a teaspoon of turmeric powder and little salt. Soak and grind coconut with one cup of warm water and extract thick milk and keep. Keep the coconut residue also. Heat four tablespoons of olive oil in a deep pan, add onions and fry till transluscent. Add red chilli powder, remaining turmeric powder, coriander powder and stir. Add green chillies, curd chillies, curry leaves and *kodumpulli*. Add the coconut residue and four cups of water. Boil till it reduces by half and thickens. Set aside.

Heat the remaining olive oil in another pan, add pounded *methi* seeds and whole red chillies and stir well. Add the marinated prawns, drumsticks and mango. Cook for two to three minutes or till the prawns are three-fourth done. Pour in the curry and simmer till it combines well. Add salt to taste. Remove from heat and add the coconut milk and let it simmer for five minutes. Serve hot.

Note: To make curd chillies, soak chillies in a mixture of thin curd and salt for 6-8 hours. Dry in sun till all the moisture dries up. Store in airtight tins. Deep-fry and use as an accompaniment also.

Main Course

CHICKEN GHASSI

INGREDIENTS

800 grams chicken, cut into 1-inch pieces
1½ tablespoons lemon juice
1½ tablespoons ginger-garlic paste
½ teaspoon turmeric powder
Salt to taste
1½ cups scraped coconut
1½ tablespoons coriander seeds
15 black peppercorns
½ teaspoon fenugreek seeds
1½ teaspoons cumin seeds
10 whole *Bedgi* red chillies, seeded
3 tablespoons olive oil
3 medium onions, chopped
½ teaspoon mustard seeds
10 curry leaves
8 garlic cloves, chopped
1½ tablespoons tamarind pulp
¾ cup coconut milk (page 79)

METHOD

Marinate chicken with lemon juice, ginger-garlic paste, turmeric powder and salt for an hour. To make the *masala*, dry-roast coconut to a light brown. Lightly sauté coriander seeds, black peppercorns, fenugreek seeds, cumin seeds and whole *Bedgi* red chillies in two teaspoons of olive oil. Grind these along with roasted coconut and half the onions to a fine paste using a little water if required. Heat remaining olive oil in pan. Add mustard seeds and curry leaves. When the seeds splutter, add garlic and remaining onions and sauté for five minutes on low heat. Add ground *masala* and sauté for five minutes till a nice aroma is given out. Add marinated chicken. Stir well and add one cup of water and adjust salt. Stir, cover and cook for ten minutes. Add tamarind pulp and stir well. Add coconut milk and remove from heat just when it comes to a boil. Serve hot.

KEEMA MATAR

INGREDIENTS

½ kilogram minced mutton
½ cup green peas, boiled
6 tablespoons olive oil
2-3 green chillies, sliced
1 teaspoon cumin seeds
2 large onions, chopped
½ tablespoon ginger paste
½ tablespoon garlic paste
2 medium tomatoes, chopped
Salt to taste
1½ tablespoons red chilli powder
1 tablespoon coriander powder
¼ teaspoon turmeric powder
½ teaspoon *garam masala* powder
2 tablespoons chopped fresh coriander leaves
Lemon wedges, to serve

METHOD

Heat olive oil in a pan, add green chillies and sauté for half a minute. Add cumin seeds and when they begin to change colour, add onions and sauté till golden brown. Add ginger paste and garlic paste and sauté for a minute. Add tomatoes and salt. Cover and cook on low heat for two to three minutes. Add red chilli powder, coriander powder and turmeric powder and continue to cook for another minute. Add minced mutton, sauté for two minutes, add half a cup of water, stir and cover and cook on medium heat for fifteen to twenty minutes till the mutton is done, water has evaporated and oil surfaces on top. Stir in the peas and *garam masala* powder and cook for a minute. Serve hot, garnished with coriander leaves and lemon wedges.

See page 158 for the recipe of *Garam Masala* Powder.

NALLI GOSHT

INGREDIENTS

800 grams lamb leg pieces
6 tablespoons olive oil
4 green cardamoms
2 black cardamoms
5-6 cloves
1 inch stick cinnamon
5-6 black peppercorns
3 bay leaves
3 large onions, sliced
2 tablespoons garlic paste
2 tablespoons ginger paste
1 tablespoon red chilli powder
1 tablespoon coriander powder
½ cup tomato purée
¾ cup yogurt
1 teaspoon *garam masala* powder
Salt to taste

METHOD

Heat olive oil in a thick-bottomed pan. Add green cardamoms, black cardamom, cloves, cinnamon, black peppercorns, bay leaves and onions. Sauté until onions are lightly browned. Add ginger paste, garlic paste, red chilli powder, coriander powder and cook for one minute. Add lamb pieces. Stir and cook for three minutes on medium heat. Add three cups of water and bring it to a boil. Simmer and cook covered on medium heat for twenty to twenty five minutes or until lamb pieces are almost cooked. Whisk together tomato purée and yogurt and add to the cooked *nalli*. Add salt and *garam masala* powder and cook covered for ten minutes. Serve hot with hot *chapatis* (type of Indian bread).

See page 158 for the recipe of *Garam Masala* Powder.

Main Course

KOLHAPURI SUKKA CHICKEN

INGREDIENTS

1 medium (approx 1 kilogram) chicken,
  cut into 12 pieces
1 teaspoon Kolhapuri dry chutney
1 tablespoon sesame seeds
2 tablespoons poppy seeds
6-8 black peppercorns
1 teaspoon caraway seeds
1 inch stick cinnamon
3-4 green cardamoms
1 black cardamom
4-5 cloves
1 blade mace

¼ cup grated dried coconut
8-10 Bedgi red chillies
1 inch ginger piece
6-8 garlic cloves
5 tablespoons olive oil
3-4 whole dried red chillies
3 medium onions, chopped
¼ teaspoon turmeric powder
A pinch of grated nutmeg
Salt to taste
2 tablespoons chopped fresh coriander leaves

METHOD

Dry-roast sesame seeds, poppy seeds, black peppercorns, caraway seeds, cinnamon, green cardamom, black cardamom, cloves and mace separately. Cool and grind along with dried coconut and *Bedgi* red chillies to a fine paste, adding a little water. Grind ginger and garlic to a fine paste. Heat olive oil in a thick-bottomed pan, add dried red chillies, stir-fry briefly, remove and reserve for garnish. Add onions to the same oil and sauté till golden brown. Add ginger-garlic paste and cook on medium heat for a few seconds.

Stir in the prepared coconut paste and cook further for three to four minutes on medium heat, stirring frequently. Add chicken pieces, mix well and cook on high heat, stirring continuously, for two to three minutes. Add half a cup of water and continue cooking on medium heat for three to four minutes, stirring frequently. Add turmeric powder, grated nutmeg, Kolhapuri dry chutney and salt. Mix well and cook further till chicken is completely cooked, stirring frequently. The *masala* (gravy) should be quite thick and dry. Serve hot garnished with coriander leaves and fried dried red chillies.

See page 159 for the recipe of Kolhapuri Dry Chutney

SABZI AUR TAMATAR KA PULAO

INGREDIENTS

1½ cups *Basmati* rice, soaked
2 small carrots, cubed
½ cup shelled green peas
¼ medium cauliflower, separated into florets
10-12 French beans, cut into ½ inch pieces
3-4 tomatoes, chopped
3 tablespoons olive oil
1 teaspoon cumin seeds
3-4 green cardamoms
3-4 black cardamoms
1 inch stick cinnamon
4-6 cloves
2 medium onions, sliced
Salt to taste

METHOD

Heat olive oil in a thick-bottomed pan. Add cumin seeds, green cardamoms, black cardamoms, cinnamon and cloves. Once they start to splutter, add onions and fry till translucent. Add tomatoes and cook till oil separates. Add salt and three cups of water and bring to a boil. Add carrots and cook for five minutes. Add drained rice to the pan. Once the mixture comes to a boil add green peas, cauliflower florets, French beans and salt. Reduce heat and cover the pan. Cook till rice is completely done. Uncover the pan when the rice is cooked and stir lightly with a spatula so as to ensure that no lumps are formed. Serve hot.

This fragrantly colourful presentation of rice with vegetables is as much a favourite on the weekly menu in my home as at parties. All you need with it is a *raita* and some roasted *papads* to make a complete meal.

ALOO ANARDANA KULCHA

INGREDIENTS

2 cups refined flour
2 medium potatoes, boiled and grated
1 teaspoon pomegranate seeds, roasted and coarsely powdered
¼ teaspoon soda bicarbonate
Salt to taste
2 tablespoons yogurt
2 tablespoons milk
4 tablespoons olive oil
½ medium onion, chopped
¼ cup chopped fresh coriander leaves
8-10 fresh mint leaves, chopped
2 green chillies, chopped
½ tablespoon red chilli powder
1 tablespoon roasted cumin powder
¾ teaspoon onion seeds
2 tablespoons extra virgin olive oil

METHOD

Sift refined flour with soda bicarbonate and salt into a bowl. Gradually mix in the yogurt and milk. Add sufficient water to make soft and smooth dough. Cover with a damp cloth and rest the dough for ten minutes. Add two tablespoons of olive oil and knead the dough well. Cover it once again and set aside for at least an hour. Divide the dough into six to eight equal portions and form them into smooth balls. Preheat the oven to 220°C/425°F/Gas Mark 7.

Grease a baking tray with a little olive oil. Mix potatoes, onion, coriander leaves, mint leaves, green chillies, *anardana* powder, red chilli powder, roasted cumin powder and salt to taste. Divide the potato mixture into six to eight equal portions and set aside. Flatten a portion of dough, place a portion of the potato mixture in the centre and fold the edges over to form a ball. Place the stuffed ball on a lightly floured surface and roll gently into a disc of four to five inch diameter. Brush lightly with a little olive oil, sprinkle onion seeds on the surface and press with your palm. Similarly make the remaining *kulchas*. Place them on the greased baking tray and bake in a preheated oven for about six to eight minutes. Brush the hot *kulchas* with extra virgin olive oil and serve immediately.

GUJARATI KADHI

INGREDIENTS

¼ cup gram flour
2 cups yogurt
1 lemon sized piece jaggery, grated
2 green chillies, chopped
Salt to taste
2 tablespoons olive oil
½ teaspoon mustard seeds
½ teaspoon cumin seeds
8-10 curry leaves
2 whole dried red chillies
3-4 cloves
1 inch stick cinnamon
A pinch of asafoetida

METHOD

Whisk together *besan* and yogurt to make a smooth mixture. Add four cups of water and mix well. Combine yogurt mixture, jaggery and green chillies. Cook, stirring continuously, till *kadhi* attains medium consistency. Add salt to taste. Heat olive oil in a small pan and add mustard seeds, cumin seeds, curry leaves, dried red chillies, cloves, cinnamon and asafoetida. When seeds begin to splutter, add it to the *kadhi* and mix well. Serve hot.

For some time after I got married to Alyona I used to enjoy this *kadhi* as a soup! Now I have learnt that it is as wonderful, piping hot, mixed with steamed rice too.

BHINDI RAITA

INGREDIENTS

10-15 medium ladies' fingers, diagonally sliced
Olive oil to deep-fry
4 cups yogurt
Salt to taste
1½ teaspoons red chilli powder
1 teaspoon roasted cumin powder

METHOD

Heat sufficient olive oil in a *kadai* (wok) and deep-fry *bhindis* till crisp. Drain and place them on absorbent paper. Whisk together yogurt, salt, red chilli powder and roasted cumin powder. Chill in the refrigerator for half an hour. Add three-fourth of the fried *bhindis* to the yogurt mixture just before serving. Mix. Garnish with the remaining fried *bhindis* and serve immediately.

MURGH BIRYANI

INGREDIENTS

500 grams chicken, cut into 1½ inch pieces on the bone

1½ cups Basmati rice, soaked

1 tablespoon ginger paste

1 tablespoon garlic paste

1 teaspoon green chilli paste

1 tablespoon coriander powder

1 tablespoon cumin powder

1 teaspoon *garam masala* powder

1 teaspoon green cardamom powder

Salt to taste

1 cup yogurt

3 tablespoons olive oil

1 bay leaf

4 cloves

2 green cardamoms

1 black cardamom

5 cups chicken stock (see below)

A few saffron threads

1 tablespoon milk

1 teaspoon caraway seeds

1 inch ginger, cut into thin strips

2 medium onions, sliced and deep fried

½ cup chopped fresh mint leaves

2 tablespoons chopped fresh coriander leaves

1 teaspoon screwpine essence

1 teaspoon rose water

METHOD

Marinate chicken with ginger paste, garlic paste, green chilli paste, coriander powder, cumin powder, *garam masala* powder, green cardamom powder, salt and yogurt for about half an hour. Heat one tablespoon olive oil in a pan. Add bay leaf, cloves, green cardamoms and black cardamom and sauté for half a minute. Add rice and sauté for a minute. Add chicken stock and bring it to a boil. Reduce heat and cook for eight to ten minutes or till the rice is three-fourth done. Drain and set aside.

Soak saffron in milk. Heat remaining olive oil in a thick-bottomed pan. Add caraway seeds and sauté. Add marinated chicken pieces and sauté for three to four minutes or till it is half cooked. Remove the pan from heat. Spread the rice over the chicken. Sprinkle saffron-flavoured milk, ginger strips, fried onions, mint leaves, coriander leaves, *kewra* water and rose water. Cover and cook on *dum* (stew in its own juices) for fifteen to twenty minutes on low heat. Serve hot with a *raita* (yogurt relish) of your choice.

Note: To make chicken stock, Boil 200 grams chicken bones in water for 5 minutes. Drain and discard water. Boil blanched bones with a roughly chopped carrot, celery stalk, leek, 2-3 parsley stalks, 6-7 black peppercorns, 5-6 cloves, 1 bay leaf and 10 cups of water.
Remove any scum which rises to the surface and replace it with more cold water. Simmer for at least one hour.
Remove from heat, strain, cool and store in a refrigerator till further use.

See page 158 for the recipe of *Garam Masala* Powder.

MISSI ROTI

INGREDIENTS

2 cups gram flour
¾ cup wholewheat flour
¼ cup chopped fresh coriander leaves
4 green chillies, chopped
1 medium onion, chopped
1 teaspoon turmeric powder
Salt to taste
1 teaspoon *chaat masala*
1 tablespoon pomegranate seeds, crushed
1 tablespoon olive oil + to grease
2 tablespoons extra virgin olive oil

METHOD

Sift together the two flours into a bowl. Add coriander leaves, green chillies, onion, turmeric powder, salt, *chaat masala*, *anardana* and one tablespoon of olive oil. Add enough water to form a soft dough. Cover the dough with a damp cloth and rest for ten minutes. Divide the dough into sixteen equal portions and form into balls. Grease your palms. Grease the tabletop and keep a dough ball on it. Press a little. Slightly dampen one palm and using both your palms pat the ball between them to make a *roti* (disc) or roll it on a lightly floured surface using a rolling pin to a disc of six inches diameter. Heat the *tandoor* (clay oven). Lightly dampen one side of the *roti* and stick it onto the *tandoor* wall. Alternatively you can roast the *roti* on a hot *tawa* (griddle). Cook till done. Apply a little extra virgin olive oil immediately and serve hot.

See page 159 for the recipe of *Chaat Masala*.

AMTI

INGREDIENTS

1 cup split pigeon peas, soaked
¼ teaspoon turmeric powder
1½ tablespoons olive oil
5-6 curry leaves
1 teaspoon mustard seeds
½ teaspoon red chilli powder
Salt to taste
2 tablespoons tamarind pulp
1 tablespoon grated jaggery
1 teaspoon *goda masala*

METHOD

Pressure cook *toovar dal* with two cups of water and turmeric powder till three whistles are given out. Heat olive oil in a *kadai* (wok). Add curry leaves, mustard seeds and red chilli powder. Lower heat and once the seeds splutter add the cooked *toovar dal*. Stir briskly to mix well. As the *dal* begins to boil add salt, tamarind pulp and jaggery. Stir in one cup of hot water and let the *dal* boil for six to eight minutes. Add *goda masala* and adjust consistency as per personal choice. Continue to simmer the *dal* for three to four minutes. Serve hot with *chapati* (type of Indian bread) or rice.

See page 158 for the recipe of *Goda Masala*.

Try this sweet and sour *dal* with hot rice and a drizzle of olive oil. A spicy *chutney* or a dab of pickle will raise it to superlative heights. Also add a crisp roasted *papad* please!

TOMATO SAAR

INGREDIENTS

5-6 large ripe tomatoes, roughly chopped
1 cup scraped coconut
6 garlic cloves
1 teaspoon cumin seeds
Salt to taste
½ teaspoon red chilli powder
2 tablespoons olive oil
1 teaspoon mustard seeds
A pinch of asafoetida
8-10 curry leaves
3-4 green chillies, slit
2-3 tablespoons sugar
¼ cup chopped fresh coriander leaves

METHOD

Grind together coconut, garlic and cumin seeds to a paste. Place tomatoes in a pan with salt and red chilli powder. Add three cups of water and bring it to a boil. Simmer for fifteen minutes and purée when it is a little cool. Heat olive oil in a pan and add mustard seeds, asafoetida and curry leaves. Add puréed tomatoes and green chillies and bring to a boil. Add sugar. Add coconut-garlic paste and mix well. Simmer on low heat for ten minutes. Adjust seasoning. Serve hot, garnished with coriander leaves.

KATHAL KI BIRYANI

INGREDIENTS

½ kilogram unripe jackfruit, cut into 1½ inch cubes

1½ cups rice, soaked

Salt to taste

4 green cardamoms

3 black cardamoms

3 cloves

2 inches sticks cinnamon

3 tablespoons olive oil + to deep-fry

4 medium onions, thinly sliced

½ teaspoon caraway seeds

1 tablespoon ginger paste

1 tablespoon garlic paste

1 teaspoon turmeric powder

1 teaspoon roasted cumin powder

2 teaspoons coriander powder

2 teaspoons red chilli powder

3 medium tomatoes, chopped

1½ cups yogurt, whisked

2 tablespoons chopped fresh coriander leaves

5-6 saffron threads

2 tablespoons milk

1 teaspoon *garam masala* powder

10-12 fresh mint leaves, hand torn

1 tablespoon screwpine essence

METHOD

Drain and parboil rice in six cups of water adding a little salt and two green cardamoms, two black cardamoms, cloves and one stick of cinnamon. Drain when parboiled. Refresh in cold water and drain again. Heat sufficient olive oil in a *kadai* (wok) and deep-fry jackfruit cubes. Drain and place on absorbent paper and set aside.

Deep-fry half the onions in the same oil till golden brown and crisp. Drain and place on absorbent paper and set aside. Heat three tablespoons of olive oil in a deep thick-bottomed pan. Add caraway seeds and remaining green cardamoms, black cardamom and crushed cinnamon. Add remaining onions and sauté for a while. Add ginger paste, garlic paste and continue to sauté. Add turmeric powder, roasted cumin powder, coriander powder, red chilli powder and tomatoes. Continue to sauté for two to three minutes. Add fried jackfruit and stir. Add yogurt, salt and coriander leaves. Soak saffron in lukewarm milk and set aside.

Preheat the oven to 200°C/400°F/Gas Mark 6. Take a large bowl, arrange half of the jackfruit mixture in it. Over this spread a layer of rice. Sprinkle saffron-flavoured milk, *garam masala* powder, a few mint leaves and a few drops of *kewra* water. Arrange the rest of the jackfruit mixture. Cover with rice. Garnish with fried onions, a few mint leaves and remaining *kewra* water. Cover with aluminum foil and bake in the preheated oven for about twenty to twenty five minutes. Serve hot with a *raita* (yogurt relish) of your choice.

See page 158 for the recipe of *Garam Masala* Powder.

Accompaniments 123

THEPLA

INGREDIENTS

2 cups wholewheat flour
½ cup gram flour
1 cup chopped fresh fenugreek leaves
¼ teaspoon turmeric powder
½ teaspoon red chilli powder
1 teaspoon ginger-green chilli paste
2 tablespoons olive oil + to shallow-fry
Salt to taste
Yogurt as required

METHOD

Mix wholewheat flour, gram flour, fenugreek leaves, turmeric powder, red chilli powder, ginger-green chilli paste, two tablespoons olive oil and salt and mix well. Add sufficient yogurt and knead into a semi-soft dough. Cover with a damp cloth and set aside for fifteen minutes. Divide into sixteen equal sized balls and roll out into thin *chapatis* (flat roundels). These are *theplas*. Heat a *tawa* (griddle) and roast the *theplas*, applying a little oil on either side, till both the sides are evenly golden. These can be eaten hot or cold.

I have yet to find a Gujarati home without *theplas*. With *chhunda* - another favourite Gujarati unripe mango relish - it is an unforgettable snack!

KALI DAL

INGREDIENTS

¾ cup whole black gram
3 tablespoons red kidney beans
3 tablespoons split Bengal gram
3 inch ginger
7-8 garlic cloves
Salt to taste
2 teaspoons red chilli powder
5 tablespoons olive oil
1 medium onion, chopped
1 teaspoon cumin seeds
3 whole dried red chillies, broken into two
1 cup tomato purée
1 teaspoon *garam masala* powder
2 tablespoons chopped fresh coriander leaves
¼ cup fresh cream

METHOD

Soak together *sabut urad, rajma* and *chana dal* in four cups of water for eight hours. Cut half the ginger into thin strips and grind the remaining piece with garlic to a fine paste. Take the soaked *dals* in a pressure cooker, add ginger strips, salt, red chilli powder and three cups of water. Close the lid and cook on high heat till two whistles are given out.

Lower the heat and cook for about fifteen minutes. For *tadka* (tempering), heat olive oil in a pan. Add onion and sauté. Add cumin seeds, red chillies, ginger-garlic paste and sauté for two minutes. Add tomato puree and mix. Add *garam masala* powder to the *tadka* and mix. Add the cooked *dals* and mash them a little. Add one cup of water and mix. Simmer on low heat for two minutes. Add coriander leaves and fresh cream and mix again. Serve piping hot.

See page 158 for the recipe of *Garam Masala* Powder.

PRAWN PULAO

INGREDIENTS

300 grams prawns, shelled and deveined
1½ cups Basmati rice, soaked
4 tablespoons olive oil
3 large onions, sliced
2 teaspoons ginger-garlic paste
2 medium tomatoes, chopped
2 green chillies, slit
2 teaspoons red chilli powder
½ teaspoon turmeric powder
Salt to taste
½ cup coconut milk
¼ cup yogurt
1 teaspoon *garam masala* powder
1 tablespoon chopped fresh coriander leaves

METHOD

Heat olive oil in a pressure cooker. Add onions and sauté till light golden. Add ginger-garlic paste and sauté for a minute. Add tomatoes and continue to sauté till the tomatoes soften. Add green chillies and red chilli powder and sauté till oil begins to separate. Add turmeric powder, prawns and salt. Sauté for two minutes and add coconut milk and yogurt. Add *garam masala* powder and stir. Simmer for two minutes on low heat. Add drained rice and stir lightly. Add two cups of water and bring it to a boil. Cover with lid and pressure cook on medium heat till two whistles. Open lid when pressure reduces, garnish with coriander leaves and serve hot.

See page 158 for the recipe of *Garam Masala* Powder.

See page 79 for the recipe of Coconut Milk.

KOKI
Flaky Sindhi Roti

INGREDIENTS

2½ cups wholewheat flour
2 small onions, roughly chopped
Salt to taste
2-3 green chillies, chopped
2 tablespoons chopped fresh coriander leaves
1 tablespoon olive oil + to shallow-fry
4 tablespoons fresh cream

METHOD

Take wholewheat flour in a bowl. Add onions, salt, green chillies, coriander leaves, one tablespoon of olive oil and *malai* and mix well. Add sufficient water to make a stiff dough. Cover and rest the dough for about fifteen minutes. Divide the dough into eight equal portions (these will be larger than you would normally take to make a *parantha*). Pat with your fingers into a thick roundel. Heat a thick *tawa* (griddle), place the *koki* on it and cook evenly on medium heat for two to three minutes on each side. Apply olive oil and shallow-fry till both the sides are light golden in colour. Serve hot.

Accompaniments

ANDHRA DAL

INGREDIENTS

1 cup split pigeon peas, soaked
2 unripe bananas, cut into 1 inch cubes
2 teaspoons split Bengal gram, roasted
2 teaspoons coriander seeds, roasted
6-8 black peppercorns
2 teaspoons scraped coconut
4 whole fried red chillies
2 tablespoons tamarind pulp
½ teaspoon turmeric powder
Salt to taste

2 teaspoons olive oil
½ teaspoon mustard seeds
½ teaspoon cumin seeds
6-8 curry leaves
A pinch of asafoetida
1 tablespoon chopped fresh
coriander leaves

METHOD

Pressure cook *toovar dal* with unripe bananas and two cups of water till three whistles are given out. Grind *chana dal*, coriander seeds, black peppercorns, coconut, dried red chillies with tamarind pulp to a smooth paste. Take a deep pan and mix together boiled *dal*, ground paste, turmeric powder and salt. Heat olive oil in a pan and add mustard seeds. As they begin to splutter add cumin seeds, curry leaves and asafoetida. Pour tempering over the *dal* and add coriander leaves. Bring *dal* to a boil on high heat, stirring constantly. Adjust consistency. Cook for two minutes. Serve hot with rice.

This *dal* is an intriguing mix of textures and flavours. Include it in your daily repertoire like I do because it tastes as wonderful with *rotis* as with rice.

LAL MIRCH KA BENARASI ACHAR

INGREDIENTS

12-15 large fresh red chillies
½ teaspoon asafoetida
½ cup mustard powder
¼ cup fenugreek powder
2 tablespoons fennel powder
¼ cup salt
¼ cup dried mango powder
1½ teaspoons turmeric powder
1 cup olive oil

Recipe courtesy:
Rajeev Matta

METHOD

Slit fresh red chillies and remove seeds. Remove the stems too. To make the *masala* place asafoetida, mustard powder, fenugreek powder, fennel powder, salt, dried mango powder and turmeric powder in a bowl and mix. Add two tablespoons of olive oil to the dry *masalas* and mix. Stuff the chillies with this *masala*. Dip each chilli in the remaining oil and keep in a sterilized glass jar. Pack them tightly by pressing. Pour the remaining oil over, close the jar and keep in the sun for a week. It is now ready to be served.

HIRVI MIRCHICHA THECHA
Green Chilli Relish

INGREDIENTS

8-9 green chillies

1 tablespoon olive oil

1 teaspoon cumin seeds

7-8 garlic cloves, crushed

2 tablespoons sesame seeds

Sea salt to taste

2 tablespoons scraped coconut

2 tablespoons chopped fresh coriander leaves

METHOD

Break green chillies with hand. Heat olive oil in a pan. Add cumin seeds, garlic and green chillies and sauté. Add sesame seeds and continue to sauté. Add sea salt, coconut and mix. Add coriander leaves and cook for three to four minutes. Put the mixture in a mortar and pound with the pestle to a coarse paste. Serve with *bhakris* (type of Indian bread).

KACHCHE GOSHT KI BIRYANI

INGREDIENTS

1 kilogram mutton or lamb, cut into 2 inch pieces

2 cups basmati rice, soaked

4 inch piece ginger

20-25 garlic cloves

2 cups yogurt

2 green chillies, chopped

2 teaspoons red chilli powder

1 teaspoon turmeric powder

Salt to taste

4-5 large onions, sliced and deep fried

½ cup chopped fresh mint leaves

5-6 cloves

1 inch stick cinnamon

5 green cardamoms

1 black cardamom

10 black peppercorns

¼ cup *potli masala*

½ teaspoon caraway seeds

½ teaspoon green cardamom powder

2 teaspoons *garam masala* powder

1 cup chopped fresh coriander leaves

½ cup hand torn fresh mint leaves

5 tablespoons olive oil

6-8 saffron threads dissolved in 3 tablespoons milk

2 tablespoons rose petals

1 teaspoon rose water

1 teaspoon screwpine essence

Dough made of wheat flour to seal

METHOD

Grind half of the ginger with garlic to a fine paste. Chop the remaining ginger into thin strips. Mix mutton pieces with yogurt, ginger-garlic paste, green chillies, red chilli powder, turmeric powder, salt, one-third of the fried onions and chopped mint leaves. Tie the cloves, cinnamon, green cardamoms, black cardamom, black peppercorns and *potli masala* in a piece of muslin to make a *potli* (bundle). Add this *potli* to a pan with five cups of boiling water. Add salt, caraway seeds and rice. Cook till the rice is parboiled. Remove the *potli* and drain the rice.

In a thick-bottomed vessel arrange half of the marinated mutton. Cover with half of the rice. Sprinkle one third of the fried onions and ginger strips. Sprinkle half of the green cardamom powder, *garam masala* powder and coriander leaves. Spread hand torn mint leaves. Pour two and half tablespoons of olive oil on top. Drizzle half the saffron milk. Sprinkle half the rose petals, rose water and *kewra* water. Repeat the layers once. Cover the vessel with a lid. Seal the lid with *atta* (dough). Cook on high heat for five minutes then lower the heat. Keep on a *tawa* (griddle) and cook on low heat for forty-five minutes. Serve hot with a *raita* (yogurt relish) of your choice.

See page 158 for the recipe of *Garam Masala* Powder.

See page 159 for the recipe of *Potli Masala*.

Recipe courtesy:
Harpal Singh Sokhi

DOSA

INGREDIENTS

2¾ cups parboiled rice
¼ cup rice
1 cup split black gram
½ teaspoon fenugreek seeds, optional
Salt to taste
Olive oil as required

METHOD

Wash both the rice two to three times, soak in six cups of water for at least four hours. Wash and soak *dal* in three cups of water also for a similar time. Add fenugreek seeds (if using) to the soaking *dal*. Drain and grind the rice and *dal* separately to a smooth texture and dropping consistency. Mix both the batters with hand thoroughly in a whipping motion. Add salt and mix again. Keep the batter in a large vessel, close tightly and rest overnight, or for about four to six hours at room temperature, to ferment. Just before preparing the *dosas* mix the batter well. Adjust to pouring consistency.

Heat a flat *tawa* (griddle) (preferably non-stick). Grease with a little olive oil. Pour a ladle full of batter and spread to as thin a pancake as possible. Couple of *dosas* may go wrong but once the *tawa* gets seasoned the rest of the *dosas* will come out well. Pour olive oil around the *dosa* and let it cook till it becomes crisp on the edges and turns golden brown. Fold and remove. You can make about twenty to twenty four *dosas*. If preparing *Masala Dosa* place about four tablespoons of potato *bhaji* (spicy dry vegetable) in the centre of the *dosa*, fold to the desired shape and serve hot.

A popular South Indian snack, this tastes wonderful with chutney but to make it more filling I recommend a dry potato stuffing. The range however is unlimited and you can substitute potato with mutton or chicken too.

PUNJABI KADHI

INGREDIENTS

For *pakoras* (dumplings)
¾ cup gram flour
1 medium onion, chopped
½ small bunch fresh fenugreek leaves, chopped
1 inch piece ginger, grated
1 teaspoon carom seeds
1 teaspoon red chilli powder
¼ teaspoon baking powder
Salt to taste
2 tablespoons olive oil + to deep fry

For *kadhi*
1 cup yogurt
¼ cup gram flour
1 teaspoon turmeric powder
Salt to taste
½ teaspoon fenugreek seeds
½ teaspoon cumin seeds
6 black peppercorns
2 whole dried red chillies, broken into two
1 medium onion, sliced (optional)
½ inch piece ginger, chopped
1 teaspoon red chilli powder

METHOD

Mix all the *pakora* ingredients, except olive oil, adding about half a cup of water. Heat sufficient olive oil in a *kadai*, drop small portions of the *pakora* mixture and deep-fry till golden brown. Drain and place them on an absorbent paper and set aside. For *kadhi*, whisk yogurt well and mix gram flour. Blend thoroughly so as to ensure that there are no lumps. Add turmeric powder, salt and three cups of water.

Heat two tablespoons of olive oil in a *kadai* (wok), Add fenugreek seeds, cumin seeds, black peppercorns and broken red chillies. Stir-fry for half a minute. Add onion (if using) and ginger and stir-fry for a minute. Add yogurt mixture. Bring to a boil and simmer on low heat for about fifteen minutes, stirring occasionally. Add red chilli powder and fried *pakoras* and continue to simmer for four to five minutes. Serve hot with steamed rice.

Standing (left to right)
Master Chef Sanjeev Kapoor, Anupa Das, Trupti Kale.
Sitting (left to right)
Rajeev Matta, Afsheen Panjwani, Harpal Singh Sokhi,
Nitin Puri, Saurabh Mishra.

BALUSHAHI

INGREDIENTS

1½ cups refined flour
¼ teaspoon soda bicarbonate
2/3 cup olive oil + to deep-fry
8 tablespoons yogurt, beaten
2 cups sugar
2 tablespoons milk
4-5 pistachios, finely chopped

METHOD

Sift refined flour and soda bicarbonate together into a bowl. Rub in two-third cup of olive oil into the flour mixture till it resembles breadcrumbs. Add beaten yogurt and knead into soft dough. Cover and allow it to rest for forty-five minutes. Divide into twelve equal portions and shape into smooth balls. Take care not to overwork the dough. Make a slight dent in the centre of the ball with your thumb. Keep the balls covered. Heat sufficient olive oil in a *kadai* (wok) and when it is medium hot, add the prepared dough balls and deep-fry on very low heat. If necessary you may place a *tawa* (griddle) below the *kadai* so that the oil does not get too hot. Gradually the *balushahis* will start floating to the top. Turn gently and fry on the other side till golden.

The entire process may take around half an hour to forty-five minutes. Drain and allow to cool to room temperature. This can be an overnight process. Heat together sugar and one cup of water till it reaches a two-string consistency. Midway through add milk to the cooking syrup so that the scum rises to the surface. Carefully remove this scum and discard. Remove the syrup from heat and soak the fried *balushahis* in it for thirty minutes. Gently remove the *balushahis* from the sugar syrup and place on a serving plate. Garnish with pistachios. Serve when the sugar has hardened.

BESAN KE LADDOO

INGREDIENTS

4 cups gram flour
1 cup olive oil
½ teaspoon green cardamom powder
12-15 cashew nuts, coarsely ground
12-15 almonds, coarsely ground
2 cups powdered sugar

METHOD

Sift *besan* through a fine sieve and set aside. Heat olive oil in a *kadai* (wok) and add *besan*. Cook on low heat for ten to twelve minutes or till *besan* is well done and fragrant. Add green cardamom powder, cashew nuts and almonds. Mix thoroughly and remove from heat. Let it cool for a while. Add powdered sugar and mix well. Shape into walnut-sized round *laddoos*. Let them cool completely before storing in an airtight container.

GAJAR AUR KHAJUR KA HALWA

INGREDIENTS

8-10 medium carrots, grated
¾ cup dates, seeded and chopped
1 tablespoon olive oil
½ cup sugar
2 cups skimmed milk
½ cup crumbled *khoya/mawa*
8-10 cashew nuts, roughly chopped
½ teaspoon green cardamom powder
8-10 almonds, blanched and slivered

METHOD

Heat olive oil in a *kadai* (wok). Add grated carrots and sugar and cook for about five minutes. Add milk and continue to cook for six to eight minutes. Add *khoya*, dates, cashew nuts and green cardamom powder and mix. Cook for ten to fifteen minutes or till almost dry. Serve hot garnished with almond slivers.

Pick the long, thin, very red, juicy and sweet carrots for best results. And for a healthier variation add dates. Not will they add to the nutritive value but also give this all time favourite dish a very interesting texture.

GUJIYA

INGREDIENTS

For outer covering
2 cups refined flour
3 tablespoons olive oil + to deep-fry

For filling
2½ cups *khoya/mawa*, grated and roasted
3¼ teaspoons desiccated coconut
15 cashew nuts, chopped
15 almonds, blanched and chopped
20 raisins
A pinch of nutmeg powder
¼ teaspoon green cardamom powder
2½ cups powdered sugar
½ cup grated chocolate

METHOD

For preparing the covering, sift refined flour and rub in three tablespoons of olive oil. Add cold water and knead into a stiff dough. Cover it with a damp cloth and set aside. Add desiccated coconut, cashew nuts, almonds, raisins, nutmeg powder and green cardamom powder to *khoya* and mix well. Add powdered sugar and grated chocolate and mix properly.

With oiled hands divide dough into small balls. Grease the *gujiya* mould. Roll out dough balls into small *puris* (flat roundels), put it on the mould and press lightly. Place the stuffing in the hollow portion. Apply a little water on the edges, close mould and press firmly. Open mould and remove extra dough. Keep *gujiyas* covered with a damp cloth. Similarly use up all the dough and stuffing. If you do not have a mould, *gujiyas* can still be prepared. Roll out *puris*, cut with a *katori* (metal bowl of four-five inch diameter) to get a proper round shape. Place stuffing on one half, lightly dampen edges and fold the other half over the stuffing and press edges firmly using a fork. Heat sufficient oil in a *kadai* (wok) and deep-fry *gujiyas* on medium heat till golden brown. Drain and place on an absorbent paper. Let them cool slightly before serving, as the stuffing inside may be very hot.

SHAHI TUKRE

INGREDIENTS

6 white bread slices
2 tablespoons olive oil
2 cups milk
4 tablespoons sugar
3-4 saffron strands, crushed
1 cup crumbled *khoya/mawa*
½ teaspoon green cardamom powder
15 cashew nuts, chopped
1 tablespoon *chironji/charoli*
A few drops of rose essence
8-10 almonds, chopped
1 sheet edible silver foi
A few rose petals

METHOD

Preheat oven to 180°C/350°F/Gas Mark 4. Remove crust from bread slices and cut each slice into two. Brush olive oil on the bread slices and bake in the preheated oven for twenty minutes. The bread will become golden and crisp. Meanwhile heat milk with sugar and saffron. Continue to simmer for twelve to fifteen minutes or till it is reduced to three-fourth its original volume. Add crumbled *khoya*, cardamom powder and half the cashew nuts and half the *chironji*. Remove from heat and set aside to cool. Add rose essence.

Arrange bread slices in a baking dish. Spoon thickened milk on them. Sprinkle almonds, remaining cashew nuts and *chironji* and bake for further fifteen minutes. Decorate with rose petals and edible silver foil and serve warm or cold.

MEASUREMENTS...

Almonds	10	15 gms
Asafoetida	1 tsp	4 gms
Baking powder	1 tsp	3 gms
Bengal gram, split	1 cup	200 gms
Black cardamoms	2	1 gm
Black gram, split	1 cup	210 gms
Black pepper powder	1 tsp	3 gms
Black peppercorns	10-12	1 gm
Butter	1 tbsp	15 gms
Caraway seeds	1 tsp	3 gms
Carom seeds	1 tsp	2 gms
Cashewnuts	10-12	20 gms
Cashewnut paste	1 cup	225 gms
Chaat Masala	1 tsp	1 gm
Cinnamon	2 inch stick	1 gm
Cloves	10	1 gm
Coconut milk	1 cup	200 mls
Coriander powder	1 tsp	2 gms
Coriander seeds	1 tbsp	4 gms
Corn flour	1 tbsp	5 gms
Cumin powder	1 tsp	3 gms
Cumin seeds	1 tsp	3 gms
Dry fenugreek leaves	1 tbsp	1 gm
Dry mango powder	1 tsp	1 gm
Egg	1 (small)	50 gms
	1 (big)	60 gms
Fennel seeds	1 tsp	3 gms
Fennel seed powder	1 tsp	2 gms
Fenugreek seeds	1 tsp	5 gms
Fenugreek seed powder	1 tsp	3 gms
Fresh coriander leaves, chopped	1 tbsp	5 gms
	1 cup	60 gms
Fresh mint leaves, chopped	1 tbsp	2 gms
Fresh cream	1 cup	200 mls
Garam masala powder	1 tsp	2 gms
Garlic	10 cloves	15 gms
Garlic paste	1 tbsp	15 gms
Ginger	1 inch piece	5-7 gms
Ginger paste	1 tbsp	15 gms
Gram flour	1 tbsp	5 gms
	1 cup	90 gms
Grated cheese	1 cup	80 gms

Grated dried coconut	1 cup	80 gms
Green cardamom powder	1 tsp	2 gms
Green chillies	10	20 gms
Green gram, split	1 cup	200 gms
Fresh green peas, shelled	1 cup	150 gms
Fresh scraped coconut	1 cup	120 gms
Honey	1 tbsp	15 mls
Jaggery, grated	1 tsp	10 gms
	1 tbsp	20 gms
Lemon juice	1 tbsp	15 mls
Mace	2	3 gms
Mawa	1 cup	180 gms
Medium-sized carrot	1	70-75 gms
Medium-sized onion	1	85-90 gms
Medium-sized potato	1	95-100 gms
Medium-sized tomato	1	95-100 gms
Milk	1 cup	200 mls
Mustard seeds	1 tsp	4 gms
Mustard seed powder	1 tsp	2 gms
Olive Oil	1 tsp	5 mls
	1 tbsp	15 mls
Onion seeds	1 tsp	3 gms
Peanuts	1 cup	200 gms
Poppy seeds	1 tsp	4 gms
Powdered sugar	1 cup	125 gms
Pigeon pea, split	1 cup	200 gms
Pistachios	10	5 gms
Red chilli powder	1 tsp	3 gms
Red chilli flakes	1 tsp	1 gm
Refined flour	1 cup	110 gms
Rice	1 cup	190 gms
Rice flour	1 cup	140 gms
Salt	1 tsp	7 gms
Semolina	1 cup	180 gms
Sesame seeds	1 tsp	4 gms
Sugar	1 tsp	5 gms
Tamarind pulp	1 tsp	5 gms
Tomato purée	1 tbsp	15 gms
	1 cup	225 gms
Turmeric powder	1 tsp	3 gms
Vinegar	1 tbsp	15 mls
White pepper powder	1 tsp	3 gms
Wholewheat flour	1 cup	140 gms
Yogurt	1 cup	250 gms

BASIC RECIPES...

GARAM MASALA POWDER

Lightly dry-roast 10-12 blades mace, 8-10 one-inch cinnamon sticks, 25 cloves, 25 green cardamoms, 10-12 black cardamoms, 2 nutmegs, 8-10 bay leaves, 8 teaspoons cumin seeds and 20-24 black peppercorns. Cool and grind to a fine powder. Makes 100 grams of *garam masala* powder.

GODA MASALA

Roast 1 cup coriander seeds, 2 tablespoons cumin seeds, ¼ cup stone flower 6 two-inch sticks cinnamon, 16 green cardamoms, 25 cloves, ¾ teaspoon caraway seeds, 15-18 black peppercorns, 10-12 bay leaves, 1 teaspoon *nagkeshar*, 2 blades mace, 3 tablespoons grated dried coconut, 1 teaspoon sesame seeds, 3 whole dried red chillies and 1 teaspoon asafoetida one by one in a little oil. Cool and grind to a fine powder. Makes 100 grams of *goda masala* powder.

GREEN CHUTNEY

Grind together 1 cup roughly chopped fresh coriander leaves, ½ cup roughly chopped fresh mint leaves and 2-3 chopped green chillies to a smooth paste using a little water if required. Add black salt to taste, ¼ teaspoon sugar and blend again. Transfer the chutney into a bowl and mix in 1 teaspoon lemon juice. You can substitute lemon juice with crushed dried pomegranate seeds or dried mango powder. In season unripe mango is a good substitute too.

RASAM POWDER

Heat ½ tablespoon of olive oil in a *kadai* and sauté 1 teaspoon asafoetida and 20 curry leaves for half a minute. Roast separately 15 whole dried red chillies, 1 tablespoon cumin seeds, 2 tablespoons coriander seeds, 1 teaspoon fenugreek seeds, 1 tablespoon roasted *chana dal*. Cool, mix and grind to a fine powder. Cool and store in an airtight container.

MINT CHUTNEY

Grind 5 cups mint leaves, 3 cups coriander leaves, 10 green chillies, 3 onions and 3 inches of ginger to a fine paste, adding a little water if required. Stir in 1 tablespoon lemon juice, salt and pomegranate seed powder.

KOLHAPURI DRY CHUTNEY

Dry-roast 1 cup coriander seeds, 1 tablespoon cumin seeds,1 tablespoon sesame seeds, 8-10 black peppercorns, ½ inch stick cinnamon, 10 cloves and 1 teaspoon fennel seeds. Set aside to cool. Roast ½ cup grated dried coconut till it turns reddish. Set aside to cool. Heat 2 tablespoons olive oil and fry roughly chopped 2 medium onions, 10 garlic cloves and 1 cup chopped fresh coriander leaves on low heat till well browned and crisp. Set aside to cool. Mix all these and grind to a fine powder. Mix with 1 cup red chilli powder. Store when completely cooled in an airtight container preferably in a refrigerator.

SWEET DATE AND TAMARIND CHUTNEY

Stone 15-20 dates and chop roughly. Dry-roast 2 teaspoons cumin seeds and ¼ teaspoon fennel seeds. Cool slightly and grind to a powder. Mix together dates, ½ cup grated jaggery, 1 cup tamarind pulp, cumin and fennel powder, 2 teaspoons red chilli powder, 1 teaspoon dried ginger powder, 1 teaspoon black salt, salt to taste and four cups of water. Cook on medium heat till it comes to a boil, reduce heat and continue to cook for six to eight minutes. Cool and serve.

CHAAT MASALA

Dry-roast 4 tablespoons coriander seeds, 2 teaspoons cumin seeds and 1 teaspoon carom seeds separately. Cool and powder them with 2-3 whole dried red chillies, 3 tablespoons black salt and ½ teaspoon citric acid. Mix in 1 teaspoon dried mango powder, 1 tablespoon salt and 1 teaspoon white/black pepper powder. Store in an airtight container.

POTLI MASALA

Mix 200 grams coriander seeds, 25 grams sandalwood powder, 35 grams dried vetiver roots, 35 grams bay leaves, 20 grams dried rose petals, 25 grams black cardamoms, 30 grams cassia buds, 15 grams cinnamon, 30 grams lichen/stoneflower, 35 grams and 25 grams and store in an air-tight jar. When you need to use it tie a portion in a piece of muslin and put it in the water to be used for cooking.

GLOSSARY...

English	Hindi	English	Hindi
Almonds	badam	Green gram, skinless split	dhuli moong dal
Asafoetida	hing	Green peas, fresh	matar
Banana, unripe	kachcha kela	Honey	shahad
Bay leaves	tej patta	Jackfruit, unripe	kachcha kathal
Bengal gram	desi chana	Jaggery	gur
Bengal gram, split	chana dal	Ladies' fingers	bhindi
Bengal gram, whole black	kala chana	Lamb leg	raan/nalli
Black gram, skinless split	dhuli urad dal	Mace	javitri
Black gram, whole	sabut urad	Mango, unripe	keri
Brinjal	baingan	Milk, skimmed	bina malai ka doodh
Broad beans	sem/papdi	Millet	bajra
Button mushrooms	dhingri/gucchi/khumb	Minced mutton	keema
Capsicum, green	hara Shimla mirch	Mustard seeds	rai
Capsicum, red	lal Shimla mirch	Nutmeg	jaiphal
Capsicum, yellow	pili Shimla mirch	Olive	jaitun
Caraway seeds	shahi jeera	Onion seeds	kalonji
Cardamoms, black	badi elaichi	Peanuts	moongphali
Cardamoms, green	chhoti elaichi	Peppercorns, black	kali mirch
Carom seeds	ajwain	Peppercorns, white	safed mirch
Carrots	gajar	Pigeon peas, split	toovar dal/arhar dal
Cashew nuts	kaju	Pistachios	pista
Cauliflower	phoolgobhi	Pomegranate seeds	anardana
Chicken breast	murgh ka seena	Poppy seeds	khuskhus
Chickpeas	Kabuli chana	Prawns	jheenga
Cinnamon	dalchni	Raisins	kishmish
Cloves	laung	Red Kidney Beans	rajma
Coconut, fresh	nariyal	Red pumpkin	kaddu
Coconut, desiccated	dehydrated coconut powder	Refined flour	maida
		Rice, parboiled	ukda chawal
Coconut, dried	khopra	Rose water	Gulab jal
Colocasia leaves	arbi ke patte	Roselle leaves	khatta bhaji
Coriander seeds	dhania	Saffron threads	kesar
Cottage cheese	paneer	Salt, black	kala namak
Cream	malai	Salt, sea	samudri namak
Cumin seeds	jeera	Screwpine essence	kewra water
Curry leaves	kadhi patta	Semolina	rawa/sooji
Dates	khajur	Sesame seeds	til
Drained (hung) yogurt	chakka	Shallots	sambar onions
Dried red chillies	sookhi lal mirch	Soda bicarbonate	khane ka soda
Drumsticks	saijan ki phalli	Sorghum	jowar
Edible silver foil	chandi ka varq	Spinach	palak
Eggs	anda	Star anise	chakri phool/ badiyan
Fennel seeds	saunf	Stone flower	patthar phool
Fenugreek leaves, dried	kasuri methi	Sweet potato	kachalu
Fenugreek leaves, fresh	methi	Tamarind	imli
Fenugreek seeds	methidana	Turmeric powder	haldi
French beans	farsi	Vetiver	khus
Fresh coriander leaves	hare dhania paatiyan	Vinegar	sirka
Fresh mint	pudina	Walnut kernels	akhrot ki giri
Ginger, dried	sonth	Wholewheat flour	atta
Gram flour	besan	Yam	suran/zamikand
Grapes	angoor	Yogurt	dahi